Joseph Blanco White

Observations on Heresy and Orthodoxy

Joseph Blanco White
Observations on Heresy and Orthodoxy
ISBN/EAN: 9783743349780
Manufactured in Europe, USA, Canada, Australia, Japa
Cover: Foto ©Lupo / pixelio.de

Manufactured and distributed by brebook publishing software (www.brebook.com)

Joseph Blanco White

Observations on Heresy and Orthodoxy

OBSERVATIONS

ON

HERESY AND ORTHODOXY.

BY

JOSEPH BLANCO WHITE, M.A.

Nunquam autem invenietur (quod quæritur) si contenti fuerimus inventis. Præterea qui alium sequitur, nihil invenit, immo nec quærit. Quid ergo? non Ibo per priorum vestigia? ego vero utar via veteri: sed si propiorem planioremque invenero, hanc muniam. Qui ante nos ista moverunt, non domini nostri, sed duces sunt. Patet omnibus veritas, nondum est occupata: multum ex illa etiam futuris relictum est.—SENECA, Ep. 33.

Reprinted from the Second Edition,

WITH A SKETCH OF THE AUTHOR'S LIFE,
From the Christian Teacher, 1841,

BY JOHN HAMILTON THOM;

THE FUNERAL ADDRESS, BY JAMES MARTINEAU;

AND

PART OF A LETTER FROM MR. BLANCO WHITE ON
"THE CHRISTIAN NAME."

LONDON:
BRITISH AND FOREIGN UNITARIAN ASSOCIATION,
37, NORFOLK STREET, STRAND, W.C.

1877.

The British and Foreign Unitarian Association, in accordance with its First Rule, gives publicity to works calculated "to promote Unitarian Christianity by the diffusion of biblical, theological and literary knowledge, or topics connected with it," but does not hold itself responsible for every statement, opinion or expression of the writers.

OUTLINES

OF THE

LIFE OF JOSEPH BLANCO WHITE.

From the CHRISTIAN TEACHER, 1841.

THE love of Truth is the highest form of the love of God. The religious affections may mislead, or they may arise from causes of a physical nature; but a pure devotion to Truth is the submission of all that is in Man to the eternal Source of Thought,—the sublime reliance of the Soul, unbribed by interest or passion, upon whatever it believes to have proceeded from that infinite Intelligence who is the Fountain of our spirits. There is no surrender to God so complete as that which is made by him who worships the Father in spirit and in truth,—whose God is Reality,—who uses no artificial means to keep up fluctuating and fluttering feelings that have no basis in his Reason, but casts all idols out of his heart, and, like Abraham stripped of his household gods, goes forth in faith to meet the untried future, knowing only that the great God has shewn him of his spirit, and that to trust in Truth is to take refuge with the Father of Lights.

The love of God in the form of the love of Truth

ensures the most genuine products of the devotional spirit;—the hope of progress, which is the root of all true humility; the practical fidelity of the conscience; and, what results from these, the trusting and childlike quiet of the heart. Christ himself has connected the sentiment of Immortality, of indefinite progress for the soul, with the worship that identifies God with Truth: "Whosoever shall drink of this water, it shall be in him a well of water springing up into everlasting life." Immortality necessarily suggests ideas of Progress; and to love and obey the Truth are the only means by which our feeble Reason can approach to the Thoughts of God. These, too, are the sources of fidelity in temptation, of sublime peace in life and death. Who steers his course so direct towards arduous Duty as he who believes that he has no safe guide but Principle,—and, when this is clear, puts away from him, as false and unfilial, all deceitful reasonings about uncertain consequences,—and feels that in following a moral Truth he is committing himself to the Love of an All-wise God? Who in the hour of agitation or death is so free from alarm of *soul*, as he whose peace with Heaven depends not on the vehemence of his belief in abstract propositions, or the chance temperature of unstable feelings, but on the sincerity with which his inward being cleaves to a spiritual God? Our Lord Jesus Christ, whose Comforter and God was the Spirit of Truth, and who described it as his mission in the world, "to bear witness to the Truth that he knew," is the one example of perfect fidelity in difficult duty, and of heavenly peace of soul in all times of trial. In the midst of a religion of prescription, and of authority, and of ritual, and of enthusiasm, and of all other substitutes for the inner communion of the soul with God, he alone, who trusted to the Truth to make him free, was established on the Rock, and could meet every crisis of his life with the strength of one supported by God—" Not my will, but thine, be done,"—and close his martyr death with the childlike trust, " Father, into thy hands I commend my spirit."

Whosoever has not the spirit of Christ is none of his. And there is no spirit so worthy to be called " the spirit of Christ" as this practical trust, this committal of ourselves to the convictions of our Reason and the monitions of our Conscience, identifying them with God who is their Source. There are causes connected with the individual mind, and altogether independent of the undue influences of society, that render unfailing devotion to Truth the most arduous form of the true worship of God, —causes arising out of the infirmities and even the tenderness of our nature,—the surrender of the mind to the prejudices of education ; the natural sloth of the intellect ; and the lingering residency of the affections amid the sentiments and images where faith first found a home. And society—which, alas! is but collective man, with all the faults of the individual reduced to system and sanctioned by numbers—society lashes us in the direction of the very tendencies which it ought to restrain, and adds the whole weight of its bribes and terrors to the difficulties which our own souls present in the spiritual work of seeking and worshipping God under the form of Truth. That tyranny of the imagination which in spiritual things fastens upon the mature mind the images of childhood; that sloth of the intellect which falls away from the toil of conceiving God, and forfeits its filial inheritance of growing access to the Parent Light; and that contraction of the affections which clings to the familiar and the known without inquiring whether it is the true, and the pure, and the holy, and the lovely,— these, which are in reality the infirmities of our nature, society has exalted into religious virtues of the highest order, and lent itself to the pernicious work of consecrating our weaknesses before God, by punishing as impiety, to the utmost of its power, every attempt to gain new light on the subject of Religion, to draw deeper water from the wells of Christ, and to think freshly of the Almighty. So totally has that portion of society which deems itself eminently Christian given up all thoughts of improvement in the knowledge of Religion, that the very supposition that there *is* anything to be added to their knowledge of God and of Christ is, in their eyes, a heresy. This is the radical evil of all dogmatic systems, that they sanctify the natural sloth and stagnation of our spiritual powers, and that they designedly excite the persecution of society against the man who reverently lifts his soul to the infinite God, and professes a faith in the possibility of new communications from His unexhausted Truth.

It is indeed most painfully descriptive of the state of Religion in this country, that an act so simple as the honest expression of opinion should, by artificial difficulties, be elevated into a rare virtue,—that in this respect it should still be with the servant as with his Lord,—and that fidelity to conscience, though not actually led to the cross, should yet have its more refined and lingering martyrdom. It would seem to be the most natural of moral occurrences, and certainly not marked with any extraordinary merit, that a man should speak as he felt, and having in simplicity sought the Truth, should in simplicity declare what he had found. But the sectarian spirit in society, the spirit of Churches under every form, has subjected to the severest temptations that simple honesty which would otherwise be a matter of course, the unprompted expression of the soul; so that the reverence for Truth which meets unmoved the frowns and seductions of that spirit, and pays its single obedience to inward conviction, deserves to be signalized, for it is rare indeed. Christians, while they profess a great regard for the truth of Christianity, have shewn very little regard for the only Christian truth a man can know anything of—*truth to himself;* and while they pray that he may be led into the Truth, they surround his path with every temptation to become a deceiver. Why was that venerable Confessor—for no less he was—whose worn remains were lately committed to the peaceful grave in Liverpool, in the presence of a few, who came to honour Truth in a Christian man, and to supply, as far as may be, with silent Reverence, the place of long familiar Love,—why was he, in his own pathetic words, in feebleness, in sickness, and in sorrow, "made a beggar for kindness"? In the name of Christian humanity, what was there in the mere circumstance of his having adopted some of our opinions, to place him exclusively within the range of our personal intercourse, and to make him a dependent on our sympathies? We think these questions *ought* to be put,—and answered by those whom they concern.* Why came he to Liverpool in the last stage of worn life to make his home with strangers? Why was he, with that noble heart so formed to love, and where he loved to instruct and bless, an almost solitary man, over whose head whole days and weeks passed in which he had no happiness but what he drew from Conscience, and only not alone because his Father was with him? Why should that which it was his Christian duty to do, be visited with such cruel penalties? Why should a change in his views of objective Truth,

---

* The writer of these notices would be doing great injustice to the friends of BLANCO WHITE who belong to the Church of England, if he produced the impression that their *affections* were alienated from him by his religious opinions. He has reason to know that their friendship and love, and generous care for him, never ceased. He would be understood therefore only to speak of the *necessities of system*, as manifested in the *facts* of Mr. White's change of condition, and separation from former friends. These necessities individuals cannot consistently set aside, so long as they are identified with the system called *Orthodoxy*, which limits Salvation to those who agree in certain opinions. He rejoices, however, to believe that, in this case, there were individuals who would forcibly have set aside everything but the dictates of inextinguishable love for a revered friend.

necessitate a change in all the circumstances of his life, and in all the daily friendships of his heart? Is this the way in which Christians express their reverence for Truth, by cruelly punishing every honest expression of it? We speak not of individuals, but of the Spirit of Systems. But this is the retributive stab which the dogmatism of the intellect inflicts upon the heart. Whoever erects himself into a Judge of saving truth, withers his own affections for all who refuse his tribunal. Those who presume to *know* God's judgments will act accordingly. They will not love those whom God does not love. And this is the social spirit of Orthodoxy!

And that these are feelings which we do not impute to him, but which actually embittered every day and hour of the last years of his life, we can produce most affecting evidence. It appears from his Journal, that on one occasion he attended in that humble burying-ground where now some of the most honoured of the earth repose, brought there by the same desire to pay respect to *humanity* which lately led others to his own grave. We will extract the record of his feelings on that occasion: it will make him known better than the descriptions of another.

"*Liverpool, January* 18, 1837.

"I am just returned from seeing a Unitarian minister* who lived near me laid in his grave. This is the only funeral which I have attended during my long residence in England: but I feared there would be few present, and I wished to

* The Rev. Mr. Perry.

shew this mark of respect to the deceased, as well as to my new religious connection. I could not prevent my tears falling while the coffin was let down. There is indeed much in my sensibility which is nervous; yet a mind so stored with baffled affections and regrets as mine, may be excused for its weakness. My efforts to suppress external marks of feeling are indeed very great, but not equal to the intended object. My tear, however, was not for the deceased personally, with whom I was not at all intimate; it was for *humanity*—suffering, struggling, aspiring, daily perishing and renewed humanity. As to the grave, and the descent of the coffin, and the strange noise of the sliding ropes—these things raise no melancholy feelings within me. I know not how soon I shall be laid in that same ground—for I have desired in my will to be buried in Renshaw Street Chapel—and the thought of my last home came vividly before me. No! it is not death that moves me; but the contemplation of the rough path, and the darkened mental atmosphere, which the human passions and interests, disguised as religion, oblige us to tread and cross on our way to the grave. What uncharitable, nay, what barbarous feelings, under the name of *religious* fears, would the view of the good and, I believe, long-tried man whom we committed to the ground, have raised in the bosom of many otherwise kind-hearted persons whom I know! What shock would my own presence have given to a multitude of orthodox persons, who, but for my secession from the Church, would proclaim themselves my attached friends! Is there no hope that the notion of Orthodoxy—that most deadly moral poison for the heart—shall be well subdued, if not totally conquered, in this country?"

And this was not the first time that this spirit had cast him, alone and friendless, upon the wide world;

his whole life was one continued struggle for Conscience' sake, and slow and weary was the obstructed way by which he forced himself forwards from light to light,— honoured and cherished by each party in turn, as long as they could boast themselves of his name, or make use of his reputation, but cast out (reluctantly indeed, and only under the necessities of system, but still cast out) as soon as, having become familiar with the ground they occupied, he saw that it was not co-extensive with the Truth of God, and attempted to enlarge its boundaries. We use his own words in the preface to his latest work:

"Convinced that it is my duty publicly to dissent from some doctrines upon which the Orthodox seem to consider themselves as incapable of mistake, (else they would not treat those that deny them as guilty of something worse than an error of judgment,) I perceived the necessity, and submitted to the pain, of quitting the domestic society of a family, whose members shewed me an affection seldom bestowed but upon a near relative, and whom I love with all the tenderness and warmth of a heart which nature has not made either cold or insensible to kindness.

"It is not my intention to court the sympathy of the public on the score of what I have had to endure on this occasion. I will not complain; though this is certainly the *second time* that ORTHODOXY has reduced me to the alternative of dissembling, or renouncing my best external means of happiness. But I humbly thank God that the love of honesty and veracity which He implanted in my soul, has been strengthened, constantly and visibly, from the moment that, following its impulse, I quitted my native country.

From that time to the present—a period of five-and-twenty years*—every day seems to have made me more and more obedient to the principle, *not to deceive either by word or deed.* To countenance *externally* the profession of what *internally* I am convinced to be injurious to the preservation and proper spread of Christ's true gospel, would be a conduct deserving bitter remorse and utter self-contempt."—*Heresy and Orthodoxy.*

It has been said that there is no sight on which the Divine eye rests with such full love as that of a good man struggling with difficulties,—a true mind seeking light. We shall aim to present this spectacle as it was with a regard for reality, which here, indeed, we are under no temptation to violate; for in this case, reality itself will require the deepest colours of the heart.

JOSEPH BLANCO WHITE, by birth and education, and, for a time, by earnest faith and clerical profession, was a Roman Catholic. Of Irish descent, but a Spaniard by two generations, he was born in Seville, unfortunately for him, the most bigoted and ascetic town in Spain; and there, from his tenderest years, he was subjected to that monastic discipline, that awful influence over the senses and the imagination, by which the Roman Catholic Church usurps the infant mind. The only object of his parental education was "to make him religious in their own sense of the word, and in perfect deference to the Priest who directed the conscience of the family."

* Written in 1835.

"Of the excellence of my parents' hearts," he says, "of their benevolence, their sincere piety, it is impossible to speak too highly. Their misfortune and my own, as far as my happiness depended on their influence, was their implicit obedience to the system of religion in which they lived and died. In accordance with what that system established as Christian perfection, they endeavoured to bring me up consistently with the models proposed by the Church of Rome. By keeping me from the company of other children, they imagined they could preserve my mind and heart from every contamination. They thus made me a solitary being during my childhood. I well recollect how I looked on the children of the poor who were playing in the streets, and envied their happiness in being allowed to associate with their equals. The theoretical part of my religious education was confined to the knowledge of the catechism, with theological explanations in the jargon of school divinity. In such explanations of mysteries I certainly became an adept for my age. The practical part consisted in a perpetual round of devotional practices, of which I still preserve the most painful recollection. I absolutely dreaded the approach of Sunday. Early in the morning of that formidable day I was made to go with my father to the Dominican Convent, where his confessor resided; afterwards we went to the Cathedral, where I had to stand or kneel for hours. Many times did I faint through exhaustion, but nothing could save me from a similar infliction on the succeeding Sunday. The day ended in visiting the wards of a crowded and pestilential hospital, where my father, for many years, spent two or three hours of the evening in rendering to the sick every kind of service, not excluding the most menial and revolting."

These ascetic practices produced their natural effect

on a child of excessive sensibility: he was wretched, but he was a spiritual captive, helpless in the hands of his directors. At the risk of dwelling too long on these early influences, which in the mysterious providence of God did not destroy, perhaps irritated into life, the seeds of the after freedom of his mind, we must add his own most instructive account of his first confession, for the sake of the light it throws on the natural elements and susceptibilities of his character.

"The effects of confession upon young minds are, generally, unfavourable to their future peace and virtue. It was to that practice I owed the first taste of remorse, while yet my soul was in a state of infant purity. My fancy had been strongly impressed with the awful conditions of the penitential law, and the word *sacrilege* had made me shudder on being told that the act of concealing any thought or action, the rightfulness of which I suspected, would make me guilty of that worst of crimes, and greatly increase my danger of everlasting torments. My parents had in this case done no more than their duty according to the rules of their Church. But though they had succeeded in raising my fear of hell, this was, on the other hand, too feeble to overcome a childish bashfulness, which made the disclosure of a harmless trifle an effort above my strength.

"The appointed day came at last when I was to wait on the confessor. Now wavering, now determined not to be guilty of sacrilege, I knelt before the priest, leaving, however, in my list of sins, the last place to the hideous offence—I believe it was a petty larceny committed on a young bird. But when I came to the dreaded point, shame and confusion fell upon me, and the accusation stuck in my throat. The imaginary guilt of this silence haunted my mind for four years, gathering horrors at every successive confession, and rising into an appalling spectre when, at the age of twelve, I was taken to receive the sacrament. In this miserable state I continued till, with the advance of reason, I plucked, at fourteen, courage enough to unburthen my conscience by a general confession of the past. And let it not be supposed that mine is a singular case, arising either from morbid feeling or the nature of my early education. Few, indeed, among the many penitents I have examined, have escaped the evils of a similar state; for what bashfulness does in children, is often in after life the immediate effect of that shame by which fallen frailty clings still to wounded virtue. The necessity of confession, seen at a distance, is lighter than a feather in the balance of desire; while at a subsequent period it becomes a punishment on delicacy—an instrument to blunt the moral sense, by multiplying the subjects of remorse, and directing its greatest terrors against imaginary crimes."—*Doblado's Letters*, p. 77.

There was not originally any strong impulse in his own nature leading him to become a Priest, but in a country where only the clerical profession have access to more than the elements of learning, his insatiable desire for intellectual pursuits, after a vain attempt to apply himself to commercial life, forced him into the Priesthood. Yet, though by nature full of devotional sensibility, and easily brought under the dominion of mere feelings, he was not made for a devotee, a religious slave; and even in the boy, Reason disturbed the supremacy of blind Faith,—and his earliest years of preparation, with the irrevocable vows of the Priesthood in the distance, were embittered by some faint visitings of that fuller light which afterwards arose upon his soul. These doubts and disturbances he suppressed, or they were suppressed for him, by the usual contrivances of an Authoritative Religion; by ascetic practices, by voluntary efforts to reduce himself under the dominion of enthusiastic feelings, and by studiously inflaming the affections and the imagination to the extinction of the reason. For a time these artificial means prevailed; knowing nothing of Religion under any other form, reared in this hot-bed of Roman Catholicism, and stimulated by his parents in every way that could subdue an affectionate heart, he at last took the vows of a Priest.

"No language," he says, "can do justice to my own feelings at the ceremony of ordination, the performance of the first mass, and during the interval which elapsed between this fever of enthusiasm and the cold scepticism that soon followed it. For some months previous to the awful ceremony I voluntarily secluded myself from the world, making religious reading and meditation the sole employment of my time. The *Exercises of Saint Ignatius* (ascetic practices of the most violent kind), which immediately preceded the day of ordination, filled my heart with what appeared to me a settled distaste for every worldly pleasure. When the consecrating rites had been performed—when my hands had been anointed—the sacred vesture, at first folded on my shoulders, let drop around me by the hands of the bishop—the sublime hymn to the all-creating Spirit uttered in solemn strains, and the power of restoring sinners to innocence conferred upon me—when at length raised to the dignity of a 'fellow-worker with God,' the bishop addressed me in the name of the

Saviour : 'Henceforth I call you not servant . . . but I have called you friend ;' I truly felt as if, freed from the material part of my being, I belonged to a higher rank of existence. . . . In vain did I exert myself to check exuberance of feelings at my first mass. My tears bedewed the *corporals* on which, with the eyes of faith, I beheld the disguised lover of mankind whom I had drawn from heaven to my hands. These are dreams, indeed,—the illusions of an over-heated fancy ; but dreams they are which some of the noblest minds have dreamt through life without waking—dreams which, while passing vividly before the mental eye, must entirely wrap up the soul of every one who is neither *more* nor *less* than a man."— *Dobludo's Letters*, p. 125.

" To exercise the privileges of his office for the benefit of his fellow-creatures," was now the exclusive purpose of his life, and he neglected no means that the Church appointed for keeping his mind within its power. But the crisis came at last. He has related it himself:

" When I examine the state of my mind previous to my rejecting the Christian faith, I cannot recollect anything in it but what is in perfect accordance with that form of religion in which I was educated. I revered the Scriptures as the Word of God ; but was also persuaded that, without a living, infallible interpreter, the Bible was a dead letter, which could not convey its meaning with any certainty. I grounded therefore my Christian faith upon the infallibility of the Church. No Roman Catholic pretends to a better foundation. 'I believe whatever the Holy Mother Church holds and believes,' is the compendious creed of every member of the Roman communion. Had my doubts affected any particular doctrine, I should have clung to the decisions of a Church which claims exemption from errors, but my first doubts attacked the very basis of Catholicism. I believe that the reasoning which shook my faith is not new in the vast field of theological controversy. But I protest that, if such be the case, the coincidence adds weight to the argument; for I am perfectly certain that it was the spontaneous suggestion of my own mind. I thought within myself that the certainty of the Roman Catholic faith had no better ground than a fallacy of that kind which is called reasoning in a circle; for I believed the infallibility of the Church because the Scripture said she was infallible; while I had no better proof that the Scripture said so, than the assertion of the Church that she could not mistake the Scripture. In vain did I endeavour to evade the force of this argument; indeed, I still believe it unanswerable. Was, then, Christianity nothing but a groundless fabric, the world supported by the elephant, the elephant standing on the tortoise? Such was the conclusion to which I was led by a system which impresses the mind with the obscurity and insufficiency of the written Word of God. Why should I consult the Scriptures? My only choice was between revelation explained by the Church of Rome, and no revelation. Catholics who live in Protestant countries may, in spite of the direct tendencies of their systems, practically perceive the unreal nature of this dilemma. But wherever the religion of Rome reigns, there is but one step between it and complete infidelity.". . . .

"Ten years of my life did I pass in this hot and cold fever, this ague of the heart, without a hope, without a drop of that cordial which cheers the very soul of those who sacrifice their desires to their duty under the blessed influence of Religion. . . . Ten years, the best of my life, were passed in this insufferable state, when the approach of Buonaparte's troops to Seville enabled me to quit Spain, without exciting suspicion as to the real motive which tore me, for ever, from everything I loved. I was too well aware of the firmness of my resolution, not to endure the most agonizing pain when I irrevocably crossed the threshold of my father's house, and when his bending figure disappeared from my eyes, at the first winding of the Guadalquiver, down which I sailed. Heaven knows that time has not had power to heal the wounds which this separation inflicted on my heart; but such was the misery of my mental slavery, that not a shadow of regret for my determination to expatriate myself has ever exasperated the evils inseparable from the violent step by which I obtained my freedom."—*Poor Man's Preservative; and Internal Evidence*, pp. 9—11.

His temporary unbelief in Christianity was only the necessary result of the view, imprinted by education, which identified Revelation with Roman Catholicism. When he came to this country he saw Christianity under other forms, not open, as he conceived, to the objections that were fatal to Romanism,—and his devotional tendencies, which had never deserted him, and had always sought a rest, rejoiced to be again under spiritual allegiance to Christ. What could be more natural than that the Church of England, that great opponent, in profession, to the radical errors of Popery, should receive the first acknowledgments of his reviving faith? It was not the doctrines which are considered orthodox that had made him doubt of Christianity; but the persecuting spirit of Popery, which he had supposed to be identical with Christianity,—and the theory of Church Infallibility. He did not then perceive, what he perceived afterwards, that the Church of England stood in fact upon the same foundations, though the ground is somewhat disguised,—that it regards Christianity as intended to reveal a system of doctrines, belief in which is necessary for salvation, whilst it provides no authorized Judge upon questions of faith, to make it certain that its own system of doctrines gives infallibly the contents of the Revelation. As long as he believed all the principal doctrines of the Church of England, he was not led to examine this essential weakness in its foundations; but the moment his study of the Scriptures had shaken his faith in the superstructure, he saw at once that it was an imperfect imitation of the Church of Rome, demanding, like it, the infallible Truth, but, unlike it, not providing the supposed infallible Judge. This is admirably explained by himself:

"Abhorrence of the persecuting spirit which made me renounce my native country is, perhaps, the most active sentiment of my heart. It was natural, therefore, that as soon as I became acquainted with the most powerful antagonist which Popery had ever met, I should cling to it with my whole heart. The Church of England was to me what I conceive the *Maltese* knights must have been to a Christian slave who had escaped from the prisons of Algiers into one of the Order's galleys. A long experience must have been necessary, both to myself and the subject of my illustration, to make us perceive that neither of our places of refuge was the dwelling of the full liberty we sought. But having originally examined the Church of England in its unquestionable character of a most powerful opponent of the encroachments of Rome, my eyes were too dazzled to perceive the essential defects of her constitution and the narrowness of her toleration, till the (political) events of the year 1829 disabused me, not without resistance and pain on my part."—*Preface to Heresy and Orthodoxy.*

He was a convert too remarkable not to be received with distinguished favour by the Church of England. He rose into rapid celebrity,—his writings enjoyed a popularity rarely accorded to works chiefly theological,—the University of Oxford, "in consideration," as it then declared, "of his eminent talents and learning, of his exemplary conduct, and of those able and well-timed publications by which he powerfully exposed the errors and corruptions of the Church of Rome," conferred on him the degree of Master of Arts by Diploma,—and if he had not made a solemn resolution, as a test of his sincerity, never to accept preferment, it is certain that the highest honours were open to him in this country, as they had previously been in Spain.

It is impossible here to trace at length the long process by which his mind came to the conclusion, that the doctrines of Orthodoxy were not scriptural. That process is recorded by himself, and will, I trust, ere long see the light.* It was a conclusion that he resisted as long as with honesty he could. Influenced by his affections, and by his desire for assimilation with those he loved, he tried every means to keep himself righ-

---

* See "The Life of Joseph Blanco White," &c. Edited by John Hamilton Thom. 3 vols. 1845.

teously within the Church of England, as he had before tried to keep himself righteously within the Church of Rome. This struggle between his affections and the more advanced views of his mind was the source of some of the severest sufferings of his life. He was not a man to follow the cold light of the understanding, unstopped by the thought of what connections it might loosen, what sympathies it might destroy. Those only who saw him intimately could believe with what wonderful humility so vast a mind made the attempt to conform himself to the desires of those he loved. In a life of nearly seventy years he took two steps, both of them in the same direction,—and the interval was filled up by his affections contending against the light that was forcing him away from those to whom his heart still clung. But neither was he a man to make these attempts for ever; enough that he paid the tribute to Christian love as long as honestly he could; as soon as the failure of all such attempts was manifest, he was prepared to take up his cross, and follow Christian Truth. The affections never were intended to make man a deceiver; and if Christian truth requires painful separations, let those answer for it who create the necessity.

It would be an insult to his simple and unworldly nature to dwell upon so poor a thing, as heightening his sacrifice, as that from an Archbishop's palace[*] he went forth, a lonely man, to contented obscurity and

[*] He had resided with Dr. Whately from the time of his appointment to the Archbishopric of Dublin.

neglect. That the worldly differences cost him a struggle, is a thought that will not even occur to any one who knew him. These were not the vulgar elements over which his true soul triumphed. No; it was the disturbance of friendship and affection that alone made his heart sink, and that, not so much for his own sufferings, as for the deeply-rooted and widely-spread religious evils that exact so many bleeding sacrifices. Though he never dissembled on religious subjects, yet "he could not conceal from himself that his horror of losing the affections of those whose hearts had been drawn closely to his own, had more than once enabled his feelings to disturb his judgment." And this was the noble victory he achieved over himself. We find the following entry in his private journal, when he saw that no longer could he truthfully surrender himself to these forced sympathies:

"Sincerely, though inconsiderately, and under the influence of unsuspected Popish prejudices favourable to the English Establishment, did I join myself to that Church. For more than twenty years have I struggled within myself against the growing objections which, in the course of uninterrupted theological studies, I found against her doctrines. But old and infirm as I am, and strongly tempted by the affections of those with whom I live in the closest habits of friendship, not to break openly with a Church with which they are so identified as to have lost their choice of keeping an Unitarian as an inmate—I feel it my bounden duty to shew, by my sufferings, to the world, how injurious to the cause of religion, of Christian charity and of *humanity* itself, that Church system must be which makes such sacrifices to the *love of truth* unavoidable to me; and imposes on them *the duty* of acting towards an unoffending friend—a friend whose promise of not attempting to proselyte they would certainly trust—with the reluctant severity which their intimate connection with the Church Establishment demands. For the sake of opening the eyes of people to the evils of this kind of orthodoxy, I trust in Heaven I should have fortitude enough to go to the stake."

Two days after this record, the step is taken, and he lands an utter stranger on the quays of Liverpool, as the nearest spot to the friends he had left which the sense of duty permitted. Then, when the high resolve of faithful conscience had achieved the deed of Duty, the exhausted heart, no longer called to act, felt more than the bitterness of death. There is something most sad, but unspeakably noble, in the first feelings committed to his private diary in that town,—the temporary sinking of the spirit when the sacrifice was made, and the excitement of high courage no longer needed:

"*Liverpool, January* 10, 1835.

"My whole life has not had moments so bitter as those which I have experienced within the last half-hour. Exhausted by the inconveniences of the sea passage last night, I laid myself down and fell asleep for a short time. I awoke in that distracted state which a sudden transition from place to place frequently occasions. Now every painful circumstance of my present situation crowded upon me, so that I could not bear up against the anguish of my heart. The whole of what had passed through my mind with such irresistible power respecting my duty, appeared like a delusion—

a dream, with my present misery for all its reality. In this state I had to write a few lines to those I have left, and I thought my heart would break. How entirely must I cast myself on God's mercy for support! Has not some martyr, when already bound to the stake, been tried by the awful impression that he had been brought there by a delusion? Was there not something of this horrible idea in Christ's mind, when, having deliberately gone to the garden 'which Judas knew,' he thought three successive times he might possibly have overrated the necessity of drinking the cup which he had now close to his lips? O may his fortitude encourage me, and his spirit strengthen me! How much indeed do I want it!"

But the true spirit is never long without the encouraging sense of God's presence. Angels came to Christ in that garden. And the promise of his Father to those who love him and keep his word, was not here unfulfilled. They came to him and made their abode with him, and never afterwards left him, even for a moment. I find the following entry made the next day:

"I am relieved from that mental distress which oppressed me. All my hopes of usefulness have revived. My sense of duty is again attended with courage to perform it. My heart is full of gratitude to God, the Father of my Lord Jesus Christ, for this support in my utmost need. Blessed be his name!"

The rest of his days, a period of more than six years, were spent in Liverpool, during which time his bodily weakness and ill health obliged him to lead a purely mental life, incessantly devoted to the highest departments of Thought,—rejoicing, whenever an interval of strength permitted, in his mental freedom, and in the firmer faith into which his soul rose, when his reason was relieved from the difficulties that had so long clouded his views of God and Christ.

In his private journal there is the following entry, on August 17, 1835:

"At no period of my life have I enjoyed moments of purer happiness than during the present. As soon as that agitating struggle... was at an end, I began to reap the reward of my determination. I am of course subject to attacks of that dejecting and distracting indigestion which has the power to cast a veil of darkness over nature. But I have learnt to distinguish between reality and this peculiar delusion. I wait till the cloud has glided off, and am all the while certain that sunshine is behind it. But never before had I perceived what happiness may be bestowed on man through the mere activity of his soul. I had to-day relieved the uneasiness and pain to which I am subject; had dressed myself, and, as has been my custom for some time past, had opened my window and seated myself in view of the heavens, to collect my mind for the daily tribute of adoration to my Maker. The mere act of directing my mind to Him, in the presence of his glorious works, filled me with an inexpressible, though tranquil and rational delight. I said to myself, What a glorious gift conscious existence is in itself! Heaven must essentially consist in the absence of whatever disturbs the quiet enjoyment of that consciousness, in the intimate conviction of the presence of God."

He has recorded the fact that from the time of his acting upon his last convictions, his living faith in God and Christ, and his consolations in Religion, were daily gaining strength. He had never been in any Dissenting place of worship, and having been always told that he could never bear the coarseness of other Dissenters, and the absence of all real devotion with Unitarians, he was for a time "afraid that he should be obliged to follow Milton's example, and abstain from public worship." He came, however, and saw for himself; and for the sake of those in the Church (of whom he thought there were many) who may suppress their doubts by the question, "But where shall we go?" his experience ought to be made known. These are his words:

"Oh that it were possible that some of my friends would 'come and see;' how much their unjust prejudices would be softened! The Unitarian worship stands on ground which all Christians hold as sacred. What strikes me most of all is, the *reality*, the true connection with life, which this worship possesses. All that I had practised before, seemed to be in a region scarcely within view. It was something which I forced myself to go through because I had persuaded myself that it would be good for the soul; yet, like an unintelligible and partly revolting charm, it only fatigued, but did not touch the mind, except here and there when the prayer descended from the clouds of theology, and did not adopt the slavish language of Eastern devotion. But here the whole worship is a part of my real life. 'I pray with my spirit; I pray with my understanding also.' May I not say, that suffering every hour from the bleeding wounds of my heart—those wounds that even my friends touch roughly—I have been already rewarded for acting in conformity with principle? I believe my faith in Christ is stronger—it has more *reality*—it is more a part of my being—not detached, loose, an appendage, hanging on, and almost in the way of real life—but, like an articulated limb, adding strength to the whole of my moral being."

He had the strongest sense of the importance of social worship as the purest means of keeping alive in the heart spiritual sentiments of God and of humanity; and, whenever his great bodily sufferings permitted, he never omitted an opportunity of seeking these connections with his fellow-men. Not many weeks before his death, he sent for the writer of these notices, early on Sunday morning, and having for days together suffered anguish which cannot be described, he said with tears, which he was too feeble to restrain,—" I wish you to ask for me the prayers of your congregation; I do not doubt the goodness of my God, nor do I believe that He overlooks me, or requires intercession; but my soul longs for religious sympathy, and I wish to feel that I am not separated from my fellow-christians, nor deprived of the consolations I have always found from social prayer."

The last result of his religious inquiries was the firmest faith in the *spirit* of Christianity as the divine guide and light of men, together with the absolute rejection of everything of a dogmatic or external nature, as essential to the salvation of the soul. And the only correction required to be passed on his latest published writings to bring them into more entire conformity with his last views of Religion, would be to strike out traces of a conventional language, clinging to him from former habits, which seemed to recognize other essentials of Christianity than the true allegiance of the soul to the spirit of the Christ. He had no toleration for the theological habit of setting snares for faith; and Christianity was to him the religion of life,—the acceptance by the heart and soul of the moral and spiritual Christ, *independently of all dogmas whatsoever.* He regarded as decidedly opposed to the direct purpose of the Christian mission, the common view that *any* speculative views are necessary to salvation. Many of his latest religious connection will differ from him in his views of the essence of Christianity; but he revolted from all orthodoxies, wherever they might appear; and having emancipated himself from older and more imposing authorities, he was not likely to yield himself up to Unitarian standards. Never was there a heart more full of moral love for Christ. Never was there a Disciple who more truly understood that Master.

He may justly be regarded as the most distinguished convert Unitarianism ever had, a convert all the more honoured for the consistency with which he has taken successive steps in the direction of the same fundamental principles; but we should very much mistake him if we deemed him one of a class, or that the word Unitarianism, as expressive of a sect, exactly describes and compasses his mind. He had taken up Unitarian views from a new position, and therefore we should expect him to carry into them new lights. In truth, it may be signally useful to observe what modification our views undergo when taken up by minds trained in other schools, and removed from some of our narrowing and partial influences. We are all in danger of exclusiveness,—of the bigotry of maintaining that a subject has no sides, no points of view, except those our little experience has presented to ourselves. We think too much in masses. There is too little of individual investigation and individual opinion. With most men, to determine what sect they belong to, gives you their whole confession of faith. When you know that they are Churchmen, or Independents, or Baptists, or Unitarians, you know all that is to be known about them. There is nothing to distinguish the individual from the class. Thus every little party lives within its own set of influences, and there is nothing to lead them to a new point of view. We ought to be alive therefore, with the expectation of new light, whenever a fresh mind looks upon our work from the vantage-ground of another position than our own. Certainly our views can be perfected only by taking them from every side; and since that is impossible to any of us singly, each individual must be invited to throw his own experience into the common stock of Truth, and out of the whole the view may be completed. We reverence Mr. White's progressive spirit too much to claim him as a partisan. Would to God that his catholic mind was claimed, as it ought to be, by the whole Church of Christ!

He had the most real and constantly operative belief in a guiding and protecting Providence, who cares for the individual, and shapes the course of events so as to fall in with the improvement or the happiness of those who seek the leadings of His Spirit. And this faith in a God intimately present to the individual is especially deserving of mention in a mind of so philosophical a character, and that would have revolted from the gross human conceptions of special interferences. He derived this belief in a Providence never absent from the individual, and which was the source to him of unfailing consolation, from the spiritual faith of Christ, that God was a Spirit, and that the soul which sought Him was ever the sanctuary of the Deity. The last words he was heard to utter on the subject of Providence, a few nights before his death, were these,—"that whatever might be the difficulties in the course of this our life, yet in the very direction of those difficulties there were circumstances that were more than compensations for any sufferings that Duty and Principle might bring,—and that though he had never doubted of Providence, he had seen this in his own case more clearly than any treatise had ever presented it to him." He had not much patience with those philosophical pretensions that aspired to clear the subject of Providence of all mysteries. To comprehend, in this full measure, the ways of God, he thought was nothing less than an attempt to define the infinite, to know the Omniscient. He was in the habit of saying, "Man must turn to the light within him, aided by its developments in Christ,—the highest, the purest, the best guide he knows. He must follow that light; he must sacrifice his selfish will to the duties which *Conscience* points out, and, forgetting the dark mystery of his existence, *use* that existence, so that if it depended upon him exclusively, the universe would be free from evil. Any conduct but this is madness." He believed that the material views of God which exist in the common mind were the greatest obstructions to true Religion, and the real supports of prevailing systems. He nourished his own soul on the sublime words of Christ to the woman of Samaria: "God is a Spirit: and they who worship Him must worship in spirit and in truth." This was his view of the spiritual God:

"Whenever the ideas of wisdom, order, love, blend together into an imageless conception, and that conception draws the soul into the Infinite, in an act of longing love after the eternal Source of our being, how pure, how tranquil, how confident is the adoration which the soul performs! Tears indeed suffuse the eyes—for the longing itself reminds us of a state of suffering, of evil, and of struggle; but the mind turns back to the business and the pains of life full of filial confidence, without a thought about acts of propitiation, about practical measures of safety against the wrath of the Idol-God of the multitude. It feels assured that *life* itself under a conscientious faithfulness to Reason, is the only acceptable service which the true, the spiritual God expects from his creatures. This is true Faith."

For a time, after his arrival in Liverpool, he was supported by the first feelings of complete mental freedom, and by the thought that, by his continued writings on Religion, he might be useful to mankind; but when increasing langour and pain took this hope from him, and nothing was left but a life of solitary meditation, an earnest desire for death came upon him,—to be taken away from this world, in which his part was finished. He had no fear of death. He had no fear of anything that was of God's ordaining. And yet he did not approve of those definite views of the precise nature of the future existence which some regard as the only source of effectual support. He thought that this partook of a material enthusiasm, and proceeded from a want of perfect trust. His feeling was, that he could trust a friend though he knew not exactly where he was leading him, and that if so, he could have no fears with his God. At the commencement of the last crisis of his illness, when his own impression was that he would not survive the day, he spoke almost in these words his latest convictions of Religion:

" In the midst of my suffering, all *the leading thoughts* are present with me. I am weak, and therefore my *feelings* overpower me. I have contributed my mite to the liberty of mankind. It is cast into God's treasury. I stand upon a rock. God's providence is carried on by the struggles of Reason against the passions. I have no doubts. I came from God, and I go to Him. There must be an infinite Source of the rationality which we know to be in us, and who will receive us to Himself."

For nearly three months he may be said to have been in a dying state, through sufferings which even those who witnessed could but faintly know, and with a patience whose amount God alone can compute. An idea of the weakness, of the condition of absolute dependence to which he was reduced, is faithfully conveyed in the words of one of his friends, "that even the tear which the expression of sympathy, or the heart's silent prayer drew from him, had to be wiped away by the hand of another." This image, properly taken from the higher forms of life, will picture the helplessness that cannot be described. To the necessities of such a condition he submitted himself with the gentleness, the humility of a child; but it was with the dignity of a child of God, who can receive no degradation from his Father's hands. With something of the unassailable greatness of Christ, when struck by a rude hand, he endured, as coming from God, with perfect simplicity, what without that feeling would have been humiliation worse than death. His filial faith was that singleness of vision which makes the whole being full of light. It was in fact the eye of his soul; he had no other way of looking upon life. It seemed to belong to the very essence of his being, and not to be liable to the disturbances that proceed from the instabilities of feeling. And all pain, all sorrow, has but a passing time; whilst where there is a spirit living and shining through them, the resulting fruits of instruction, the weight of glory, remain and are eternal. The suffering, the long probation, was one of the things that are *seen and are temporal;* himself, the noble spirit, is with *the unseen and eternal.* The long watch is closed. The chamber of death, which his presence made a spiritual temple, is silent now; and "the light which was with us for a while" is withdrawn into the heavens.

Among the last words that he had strength distinctly to utter were: "God to me is Jesus, and Jesus is God,—of course not in the sense of divines." "When the hour shall come, my soul will be concentrated in the feeling, 'My God, into thy hands I commend my spirit.'" A few hours before death, to the friend who was watching by him in the early morning, he said with a firm voice, "Now I die." The long struggle ended so peacefully that the moment of death was not apparent. He died on the 20th of May, 1841, at Greenbank, near Liverpool, in the house of Mr. Rathbone.

We have not spoken of his writings; of his vast intellectual power; of his ripe knowledge; of his imagination, so bold and easy, yet ever so instructive and wonderfully true; nor of his extraordinary command, the most perfect ever acquired by a foreigner, over all the resources of our language; these will manifest themselves: we have preferred to speak of what were the daily sources of his mental life and peace,—of his affections,—of his noble simplicity,—of the infinite value he attached to that sympathy which the world cannot buy,—of his views of man's discipline,—of his childlike rest on God.

That the struggle between his affections for those who could not retain him in communion, and his yet higher love for the God of Truth and Light, was the source of his chief mental sufferings, and indeed the key to the character of his mind, is apparent even from his very latest writings. The following truly sublime prayer is one of his last compositions:

"O thou great Being, who from the dawn of my reason didst reveal thyself within my heart, to Thee I may venture to speak humbly but freely, in the sanctuary of my soul. It is *there* that I obtain the nearest approach to Thee: there alone I know Thee face to face, not in the figure of a man, not in the coloured shadows of imagination, but in the truly spiritual character of Knowledge, Power, Will, Consciousness. Thou hast identified me with Thee; and yet infinitude lies between us. Thus mysteriously united and distinct, a mere thought undraws the spiritual veil of the oracle to which Thou hast consecrated me a Priest; I am instantly conscious of thy presence. No fire or thunder, no smoke weltering in the flames, no sound of the trumpet from the summit of a blazing mountain, can so surely attest that nearness. Thy 'still small voice' penetrates my very essence, and I reverence Thee from the mysterious centre where my Being and my Nothingness unite. How great, how little I am! less than dust and ashes; nobler than the morning star by my powers of Thought,—though not a breath of life is properly my own, yet I can confidently pour the workings of my heart into thy infinite bosom; nay, those spiritual workings which I call mine seem to proceed from Thee. What, if in passing through me they become subject to obscurity and distortion? I will every moment refer them back to the eternal, immutable Light which is their source, and much of the distortion will cease.

"Nor shall I be deterred because other men tell me that these very thoughts are grievous offences in thy sight. To exert my mind under a vehement desire that my thoughts may conform with Thine, is the only form of worship in my power not unworthy of Thee. Eternal Spirit! I am thy child: to trace and to increase in myself a likeness to my Father, is bliss unspeakable. This is what I would purchase with ten thousand lives: this is that which I have but one way to accomplish: a way which Thou didst shew to one, who in spite of many imperfections did ardently love Thee, and was frequently taught by Thee: I must, 'with open face beholding as in a glass the glory of the Lord, be changed into the same image from glory to glory, as from the Spirit of the Lord.' Strange! that I am invited to approach thy glory with open face, and yet my fellow-creatures would abash me when I frankly manifest my thoughts to them! Oh! there are spots on this earth, on which were I to declare to men what I do not endeavour to disguise before Thee, my life would fall a sacrifice to their indignation. Alas! this weight of misery which crushes me while I am slowly and painfully recording the thoughts I now address directly to Thee, what is it but the result of the treatment I have received from my fellow-christians, my fellow-countrymen, my own flesh, my dear friends? They thought Thee too remiss in avenging my freedom. Let them, however, be zealous for Thee in the manner most opposed to thy dealings with me. Thy internal blessings (may I not say external too?) have been multiplied in proportion as I have gained confidence to let my soul appear before Thee, without attempting to disguise myself from myself; in proportion as I became *practically* convinced that a *lie* can under no circumstances be agreeable to Thee, that man cannot serve Thee with a *lie*. What I do at this moment is the natural and unsought-for result of the growth of my reverential openness towards Thee. It is delightful to open my heart before Thee, O Eternal Being! Men will not bear to hear me; a very few who may have undergone the fiery preparation through which I have passed, may fearfully listen; and for those I record my meditations. But the madness of the mass of zealots is such, that they will not bear another man to differ from them. Their pride is fired up at such boldness. 'Think like myself—or I will make you suffer to the whole extent of my power.' In spite, O God! of thy visible conduct, in spite of that divine forbearance with which Thou treatest them when they most differ from thy best known attributes, they proclaim to the world that Thou art the most jealous and intolerant of Beings: that Thou wouldst turn thy hot anger against every one who doth not punish those within his reach whom he chooses to call thine enemy. I shall be to them a blasphemer. Ah! who blasphemes but he who calls Thee (O Fountain of Goodness!) jealous? No, Father! Thou wilt not be jealous of such a worm as Man. Thou wouldst not be jealous if there existed a Lucifer, Son of the Morning, to be something like a rival to Thee! Thy goodness would conquer him by Love."

One word more is due, not indeed to man but, to God who knoweth the heart. Neither our veneration, nor our love, must make us forget the perfection that God requires. The best men, especially, must be tried by those holy standards to which their very virtues shew their own humanity might aspire. If, then, in that noble life there were any of the errors of our human frailty,—though they left no stains upon the soul, though they had their source in no evil feeling, though their traces could not be found,—yet for erring man we claim no perfection except such as contrition and humility of soul may give,—and whilst we bless our God for the goodness and greatness which we felt and knew, we leave it to Omniscient Mercy to reckon the deductions.

We rejoice to say there are memoirs, and materials of biography, in which many noble truths are worthily inscribed, and from which many an instructive lesson may be gathered. These indeed will ill supply the living light which is extinguished amongst us. A standard-bearer is fallen in our Israel; and the wisest, the noblest, the tenderest mind amongst us, is with us no more. How poor seems now the love we paid him! How strange seems now our neglect to feed our lamps at that full light! But lately, and the amplest knowledge, the kindest and mightiest aids that one mind can give another, were within the reach of any one of us, and now the opportunity is gone, and we are left to ourselves. Will the warning never reach our hearts: "Yet a little while and the light is with you: walk while ye have the light, lest the darkness come upon you"?

Mr. White was interred on Monday, the twenty-fourth of May, in the burying-ground attached to Renshaw-Street Chapel, Liverpool.*

The following Address was delivered on the occasion by the Rev. James Martineau.

Funeral Address.

It is finished. Another term of probation has expired. Behold, a mortal rests; a friend is gone; a spirit retires behind the veil; the lonely takes his shelter within the

---

* A Monument, with his portrait in bas-relief, was placed in the Chapel by the late Mr. Rathbone, one of whose family he was for the last three months of life.—J. H. T., 1877.

upper family of God. How still and peaceful is this moment, when the long struggle of life resigns its victim, and that deserted frame lies there in silent answer to the sufferer's prayer, "O Lord, how long?" The throb of pain is felt no more; the weight of weariness is lifted off; the tension of the tortured will is quite relaxed: and of this we will speak with thanksgiving, though else it were sad that the patient light of those looks is quenched, and the accents of that venerable voice have ceased. Not often indeed can the grave bereave the world of such a priceless treasure as this: no common soul dwelt within that lifeless form: a vast knowledge, a rare wisdom, a rich experience, a devout trust, are plunged into the unfathomable night, and hidden from our eyes: yet here is death a thing divine,—"a secret place of the Most High," full of mildest protection,—a cool "shadow of the Almighty" to the fevered and afflicted mind. Physical anguish extorts from us here a confession, true also in a sublime moral sense, that it is more awful to live than to die. How, indeed, can we stand here, in the presence of that poor dust,—how perceive the fresh light and breath of morning, and the stir of labour, and the looks of living men, and all the eddies of our life-stream, flowing and whirling around it in vain,—without owning that *to be* is deeper and more solemn than *not to be;* to be awake with our Free-will, than to sleep beneath Necessity; to be ordered on to this mighty theatre of wonder and of duty, than to be summoned from it, where the wicked cease from troubling, and the weary are at rest. Ours truly is the fearful lot, to whom remains the unfinished race, the untouched burthen, the yet fierce temptations of life,—its ambushed conflicts, and its doubtful victory. On us too, as on the faithful who have gone before, may God have pity in our day; and number us with those whose peace is sealed, whose rest is sure!

Meanwhile, it is a weighty moment when we bid adieu to a mind like that which now waves to us the mortal farewell. But for the dear prisoner himself, emancipated now, we might begrudge that higher world, rich already with the accumulated spoils of earth, this new treasure from our sphere, where such spirits are all too few; and complain of that law of spiritual attraction, by which holy things gather themselves together in this universe of God:—so that to them who have much, yet more is given, and from those who have little, is taken away even that which they have. For in the fall of this life, it is not any solitary mourner, not any domestic group, not any province or any sect,—but an era of the church and the world, one of whose lights is extinguished, one of whose choice spiritual forces is spent. We part from one who has not simply *passed through* his allotted portion of time, but who has truly *lived*; sharing its most vivid existence, and in contact with its most brilliant points, and himself impressing a new form on some of its highest interests; who had gathered most of its wisdom, and experienced all its severities; who consecrated himself to the pure service of Truth, and the untiring quest of the living God, with the singleness of a great purpose and the dignity of a high faith; and in his fidelity to this vow, passed from exile to honour, and from honour back into neglect, with the courage of a martyr and the simplicity of Christ. His part is over; his work remains. The meditations of wisdom, and the sanctities of conscience cannot perish under the providence of God; and he has left us many a deep and sacred thought,—many an image from his own true soul,—for which the world will be happier yet, and the pure light of devout and Christian reason, wherein he lived, open over us a deeper heaven than the storm-clouds of fear and superstition now permit us to behold. While the labours of his mind still survive, to share the noble strife through which all things great and good must pass to their triumph in this world, he is gone where no error can mislead, no falsehood prevail, no tempest of deluded passion beat upon the good.

Our departed friend here lays down a life of *thought* and *suffering*, rather than of *action*. Such a life we instinctively conceive to be in spiritual sympathy with heaven; and the belief attests the natural feeling of all men, that the inward spirit has a divine ascendency over the outward forms of existence. We part from one who dwelt indeed within our days, but was not limited to their range; who had collected the thoughts of every age, and lived in communion with all generations of the wise. Belonging to no time, he comes before our conceptions as ripe for eternity:—the wisdom from above does but return home when it goes thither. He has but joined the great and holy with whom he has long been familiar, and entered the mild converse with immortals, long studied in exile here. He is gone to that Messiah whose mind he so well understood, and so simply obeyed; gone to the closer embrace of that Infinite Spirit, within whose Fatherhood he reposed like a suffering and trustful child. And though his mortal remains rest not in the tombs of his fathers, but in a foreign clime; yet all lands are near alike to heaven, and the pure spirit is nowhere alien in the universe of God. Let us, then, consign these relics with faith and reverence to the earth; in hope to meet their departed spirit, when we shall have crossed the gulf of silence, and reached the sphere where doubts shall be resolved, and the mystic secret opened, and the tears of mortal grief for ever wiped away.

SONNET.

By Joseph Blanco White.

Night and Death.

Mysterious Night! when our first Parent knew
  Thee, from Report divine, and heard thy Name,
  Did he not tremble for this lovely Frame,
This glorious Canopy of Light and Blue?

Yet 'neath a Curtain of translucent Dew,
  Bathed in the rays of the great setting Flame,
  Hesperus with the Host of Heaven came,
And lo! Creation widened in Man's view.

Who could have thought such Darkness lay concealed
  Within thy beams, O Sun! or who could find,
Whilst Fly, and Leaf, and Insect stood revealed,
  That to such Countless Orbs thou mad'st us blind!
Why do we, then, shun Death with anxious Strife?
If Light can thus deceive, wherefore not Life?

OBSERVATIONS

o

HERESY AND ORTHODOXY.

DEDICATION.

TO THE UNITARIANS OF LIVERPOOL.

My Respected Friends,

If, when the work to which I now have the honour of prefixing your name first appeared, I had possessed my present full knowledge of you, I should not have to regret that the token of respect and esteem I now offer you has not the attraction of novelty to recommend it. Yet I can enjoy the satisfaction that, since a second edition of this work has long been called for, I am not attaching your name to an ephemeral pamphlet. I do not feel, however, the slightest touch of vanity in alluding to the favour hitherto shewn to this small treatise; for, being perfectly aware of the cause of my success, I cannot be proud of it.

I know that the only advantage I possess in treating the subject of Heresy and Orthodoxy, is my own long and painful experience in religious matters; an experience which has been obtained on the indispensable condition of all progress—the commission of mistakes, and the painful operation of retrieving them.

Another excuse for the liberty I take in this dedication is, that but for you, my Unitarian friends of Liverpool, this second edition would have been delayed for an indefinite period. It was my desire that the reappearance of this work should not take place till after my death—an event which, as it must be known to most, if not all of you, has been more or less immediately expected during a distressing illness, which will soon be of two years' continuance. In the expectation of my final deliverance from suffering, I finished, on the 27th of October, 1837, the revisal of a copy which I committed to the hands of a dear friend, one of your Gospel Ministers. In those faithful hands it would have remained, together with my Autobiography—a work which must be posthumous—had it not been for the strange attack which certain clergymen of this town, urged by the bitter zeal inseparable from the notion of Orthodoxy, thought it, no doubt, their duty to make upon all Unitarians. A challenge appeared in the journals of Liverpool, in which it was declared that we are out of the pale of Christianity; that our theological opinions must be the result of gross ignorance or dishonesty—perhaps of both; with many other insults, couched in the language of professional sanctity. Thus Unitarians were devoted, to the utmost extent of the accusers' influence and weight, to the mixed execration and contempt of the public.

The nature and practical consequences of an enthusiastic sense of personal infallibility are too familiar to me that I should feel more than a transient pang whenever a fresh instance of this kind of persecution presents itself. I confess that the proclamation of the Liverpool crusade had no other effect when it reached my secluded sick chamber: my first wish was, that the spiritual champions should have the field to themselves; that they might enjoy their imaginary triumph among a crowd of predetermined admirers, an audience ready to subscribe to whatever their preachers might be willing to assert. I was sure that, in similar cases, the whole travail of the mountain will end in a declamatory repetition of arguments which have been thousands of times proposed, and as many times answered. I felt confident that none of the Unitarians who have taken pains to examine their own religious principles could be taken by surprise; that the clear and rational doctrines to which they have been long accustomed, would not be shaken by the dizzy mysticisms or the hollow metaphysics of our adversaries.

Our religious ministers, however, judging more deliberately and maturely than my circumstances demanded of me, resolved to accept the challenge, though, with great good taste, they declined the proposed exhibition of controversial *pugilism* upon a platform.

With the general result of this determination I believe you may be highly satisfied. On our side, productions have appeared, which, though written on the spur of the moment, shew a vitality of intellect, a logical power, an acquaintance with the philosophy of mankind (the only sound basis of theological knowledge), a familiarity with early ecclesiastical history, a power of eloquence, a dignity, an unflinching honesty, a command of temper under insults, which may justly make us proud of our leading religious instructors. There may be no accession to our numbers: converts to Unitarianism are not easily made; for Unitarianism must be the result of mature reflection, deliberate study, and strength — above all, that trust in a deliberate judgment which constitutes strength of character: proselytes only flock where the mass of mankind will always rush—to the various forms of religion which excite the imagination, appeal to the selfish passion of fear, and chime with the vulgar impressions concerning spiritual things, which are almost universally made the ground of infant education. Unitarianism does not court proselytes; on the contrary, if any persons suffering incurably from that mental weakness which requires the support of a Priesthood should exist among us, I am sure that all true Unitarians would be most glad to see them occupying their natural station at the feet of their proper Gamaliels.

Having had time to reflect on the character of the Sermons which, to judge from the noise and pomp of their first announcement, were intended to crush Unitarianism for ever, I cannot but be convinced that they have done more for our peculiar belief than even the admirable answers with which they have been met. I do not intend to write a review of that heterogeneous collection, both because such a review would require a large volume, and because the individual compositions cannot be classed so as to admit of a general estimate. Some are full of tricks unworthy of the place whence they were delivered; others are miserably weak, but respectable; in one or two there appears a steady and not uninformed mind, which is betrayed by and sinks under an untenable proposition! Only one is intended to dazzle by a display of Greek criticism; but it happens to be quite irrelevant to the question. It has so thoroughly the air of an old self-inflicted Long-Vacation task, that I am strongly tempted to think that the Liverpool crusade may have been got up for the purpose of giving an air of seasonableness to a lucubration which had been born totally after its time—that is, about thirty years later than the actual state of things might have excused it. With Unitarianism in general it certainly has nothing to do, however at a former period it might have affected the scholarship and tenets of the late Mr. Belsham. English Unitarians must smile at the obstinacy with which the "Improved Version" has been identified with them and their opinions. The preposterous character of this identification I can prove in my own case. It is about twenty years since, being full of doubts on the doctrines of the Trinity, I examined the "Improved Version," was dissatisfied with it, and put it aside. But a daily study of the original New Testament, continued for a long period, ended in making me a Unitarian, and completed my mental emancipation. I thank God for it.

I repeat my conviction that the Unitarians, not only in this town, but wherever the controversial Sermons, and more especially the *Letters* of the challengers, may be read, must eventually gain by this otherwise odious contest. Through the warning impression which the narrow and unsocial spirit of Orthodoxy will make upon them, they will perceive the necessity of utterly eradicating whatever remnants of that spirit may lie disguised in their hearts. There are many who profess Unitarianism under the false notion that the rejection of the doctrines concerning the Trinity is the last legitimate result of that mental impulse which led their ancestors to the Unitarian system. Great intolerance may lurk under this mistake. The rejection of the Trinity is but one of the more advanced consequences of the Protestant principle—the asserted right of private judgment—without which the Reformation would be only an impious rebellion. Whoever among us shall say, " We have done enough ; we must not look beyond the point at which our predecessors stopped,"— renounces every title to mental freedom, and cannot consistently remain out of a regularly *articled* Church ; nay, he is bound to join— I will not say, the *only true* Church, but the only Church which is a *Church truly,* the only Church which really answers to the fundamental point of the deceitful theory. All other Churches are lame imitations of the Roman Catholic Church : that most surprising instance of perfect consistency in error. Let us not be deceived : any church or congregation whatever, whose members believe that Christianity necessarily consists in the admission of certain facts or doctrines as immediately received from God, and in no degree partaking of human uncertainty, —any one who makes eternal happiness depend upon the unhesitating acceptance of something called revelation, and as such miraculously exempted from every one of those grounds of doubt which are inseparable from historical narratives and inferential doctrines,—any one who believes this, is rationally bound to seek for a living oracle; for without such a supernatural judge his system of saving faith is a mere fallacy.

The common plague of the Christian world is the wish to find a source of absolute certainty; in a word, *Orthodoxy*. There cannot be peace among Christians till the hollowness of all pretensions to supernatural certainty shall be fully exposed. Unitarians are certainly the nearest to a full insight into that pernicious mistake; but although the premises of the desired conclusion are almost self-evident, I cannot feel confident that the conclusion itself is general amongst us. It is, I conceive, opposed by a confused notion that the admission of the fact, that neither the authenticity of the Scriptures, nor the purity of the text, nor much less the sense of difficult passages, can be known beyond all doubt, leads necessarily to the rejection of Christianity. If this were true, the dreaded consequence would be inevitable. In vain have divines exerted their ingenuity to invent a theory for the transmission of divine truth to man, in which the first link of the chain let down from heaven to earth should be free from man's weakness. In every such attempt they have closed their eyes to the facts—1st, that a divine revelation made in human language must contract all the imperfections of that vehicle—that when the *word of God* passes through the *words of man*, it must necessarily become human:

2nd, that all historical attestation is subject to the doubts from which human witnesses and human documents cannot be exempt. The probabilities may be high in their favour; but they cannot rise above the rank of *probabilities*. In vain are we referred to miracles contained in books; for the *probability* of the miracles depends upon the *probable* authenticity of the books, and the *probable* sufficiency of the witnesses. Unless the books themselves had the perpetual power of performing miracles, their testimony, however valuable, must be *human*. These are the established laws of God; such is the nature which God has given to testimony, and to the minds which testimony has to influence. Divines have seldom or never examined these laws attentively; and hence the mistake of applying the *supernatural* remedy against doubt, in the wrong place.

In my work on *Heresy and Orthodoxy*, I have conducted my argument in total independence from the question on Infallibility and Inspiration. I have examined the New Testament in the usual light, and have shewn that it does not make Christianity depend on Orthodoxy. I have even noticed one or two of the incidental passages which, interpreted according to the deep-rooted intolerant habits of Christians, seem to demand a profession of articles of faith. In strict conformity with the true rules of interpretation, I should not have gone into these details. If a creed were of the essence of Christianity, such an important fact would not be consigned to one or two straggling allusions. I say the same of that Inspiration which is made the ground of infallibility in the writers of the Old and the New Testament. If these were FACTS, they would be the very basis of the religion of the Christ; and, as such, would stand prominent, clear, unquestionable. Such things could not be left to INFERENCE, much less to incidental allusions. Whoever wishes to escape from the meshes of the minute and hair-splitting interpretation which prevails in England, must fully imbibe the spirit of the principle I have just laid down. Those miserable battles of texts against texts, so common in English controversy, make theology almost ridiculous.

As I am not acquainted with any popular book upon this most important subject of Orthodoxy and its rival, Heresy, I have thought it advisable to enable all inquirers into religious truth, and especially you, my Liverpool friends, whose peace of mind has been assailed by a zeal not according to judgment, to make use of the results of my long meditations and my dear-bought experience concerning the source of this hot and ungovernable intolerance. Nothing but a heartfelt desire of being serviceable to the cause of religious freedom could have induced me, in my present deplorable state of health, to undertake the labour of a second revision, during which I have considerably corrected and enlarged the present treatise. May God prosper my endeavours!

Accept, in conclusion, the friendly offering of my exertions, and charitably excuse the many faults to which extreme bodily weakness exposes me. I shall, at all events, enjoy the satisfaction of having publicly and solemnly attested the high respect and esteem which I feel for you in a body, and the gratitude and affection with which I regard several Unitarians of Liverpool, with whom it is my great happiness to have established a personal friendship.

I am,

My highly respected Friends,

Your Servant and Brother,

JOSEPH BLANCO WHITE.

Liverpool, March 29th, 1839.

P.S.—As the date of the preceding letter may appear inconsistent with the collective judgment I have expressed in it, of the discourses both of our friends and adversaries (for many of them were published at a subsequent period), I am bound to explain this fact. It should be known that my corrected copy was sent to London for publication at the beginning of last April; but, without any fault of mine, the printing has been delayed many months. This unexpected delay having, however, given me the opportunity of seeing both the series of the contending Lectures, I have altered the passage in which I stated my judgment only concerning that portion which had appeared by the end of last March. J. B. W.

Liverpool, October 11*th*, 1839.

PREFACE TO THE FIRST EDITION.

THE publication of the following Letters has been prepared by a most painful sacrifice of happiness on the part of the writer. Convinced that it is my duty publicly to dissent from some doctrines upon which the Orthodox seem to consider themselves as incapable of mistake (else they would not treat those that deny them as guilty of something worse than an error of judgment), I perceived the necessity and submitted to the pain of quitting the domestic society of a family, whose members shewed me an affection seldom bestowed but upon a near relative, and whom I love with all the tenderness and warmth of a heart which nature has not made either cold or insensible to kindness.

It is not my intention to court the sympathy of the public on the score of what I have had to endure on this occasion. I will not complain; though this is certainly the *second time* that ORTHODOXY has reduced me to the alternative of dissembling, or renouncing my best external means of happiness. But I humbly thank God, that the love of honesty and veracity which He implanted in my soul has been strengthened, constantly and visibly, from the moment that, following its impulse,

I quitted my native country. From that time to the present, a period of five-and-twenty years, every day seems to have made me more and more obedient to the principle, *not to deceive either by word or deed.* To countenance *externally* the profession of what *internally* I am convinced to be injurious to the preservation and further spread of Christ's true Gospel, would be a conduct deserving bitter remorse and utter self-contempt.

It has been urged by persons whom I believe incapable of recommending dissimulation, and who have besides expressly acknowledged to me the duty of obeying conscience, that the step I had resolved to take would destroy what, in the language of partial affection, they called my former usefulness. I can easily explain to myself this suggestion, from the nature of that religious belief which, being chiefly or in a great degree supported by *fear* of a great sin, supposed to be attached to certain *heresies* (as they are called), prevents even the ablest men from going through a *free* and *impartial* examination of those subjects. As if it were incredible that any reasonable man could give his assent to such theological views, my excellent and kind advisers seem to have believed me under some mental *delusion;* else they would not have urged motives which ought not to have the least weight against *conviction.*

Unconscious, however, as I am of anything like delusion, but, on the contrary, enjoying the full and calm satisfaction which an evidence, long resisted by mere FEELING, is apt to produce when the mind honestly surrenders itself to its power, I feel no anxiety about consequences. I commit my past services in the cause of Truth (whatever they may be) to the care of that Providence, which, if in fact I have been useful, must have employed me, though an humble instrument. Of *consequences* we are very incompetent judges: on *principles* alone can we depend with confidence and certainty. If the consideration of *usefulness* could be allowed in my case, SPAIN, my native country, would long, long since, have had my services. But *dissembling*, whether in deference to *Transubstantiation* or the *Athanasian Creed*, is equally hateful to me.

Yet, why any real good of which I may have been the occasion should be destroyed by a fresh proof of my love of honesty and fair dealing, is what I cannot conceive. If anything could invalidate or weaken the force of my testimony in regard to the corruptions of Popery, it would be my SILENCE in favour of what I deem other corruptions. The great *Chillingworth* would have added weight to his unrivalled works if he had not permitted his subscription to the Thirty-nine Articles to remain in full force, when neither his judgment could approve of it, nor his natural honesty conceal his change. As to myself, I have not enjoyed any of the temporal advantages of Orthodoxy; and it is well attested that, at a time when I might conscientiously have taken preferment, I solemnly resolved never to accept it. But, having subscribed to the Articles for the mere purpose of qualifying myself for the *occasional* performance of clerical duties, I feel bound modestly to recall that subscription before my death, and to declare that I am satisfactorily convinced not only that the DOCTRINE OF THE TRINITY is not scriptural, but also that the whole *Patristical* theology, which makes up the greatest part of the Thirty-nine Articles, consists of groundless speculations which could never have obtained currency among Christians without the aid of a false philosophy. I profess Christianity as a UNITARIAN; acknowledging ONE GOD IN ONE PERSON, and Jesus of Nazareth as my guide to *his Father* and *my Father, his God* and *my God.*

In announcing such changes of views, it is usual to state *how* they have taken place. To describe, however, the circumstances of my case fully, would require a work much larger than the tract which affords me the opportunity of making my sentiments known. Such an undertaking is quite beyond my present strength. How long, how earnestly, and I may add (for who except God can know it better than myself?) how conscientiously, I have examined the whole Patristical theology, of which the Articles of the Church of England are a summary, will be known, *in detail,* when the SKETCH OF MY MIND IN ENGLAND may happen to see the light. Out of respect, however, to such persons as may take an interest in the subject, I will mention—(1) That my doubts of the truth of the established views began with the systematic and devout study of the Scriptures which I undertook in 1814, when, free from the literary engagements which in the service of England as well as of my native country had occupied me during the four preceding years, I removed to Oxford, for the exclusive purpose of devoting myself to theology. In the year 1818 (as it may be distinctly proved by the journals I kept at that time, and which are still in my possession), I arrived at the Unitarian view of Christianity; but the perfect obscurity in which I was living, and the consideration that I had not then published anything, except in Spanish, appeared to me a sufficient ground for not making a public avowal of my conviction. (2) Having, till about 1824, continued in that state, and, in spite of difficulties resulting from the notion of Orthodoxy, faithfully attached to Christianity, a revival of my early mental habits and of those devotional sentiments which are inseparably connected with the idea of intellectual surrender to some church, induced me again to *acquiesce* in the established doctrines—not from conviction, not by the discovery of sounder proofs than those which I had found insufficient, but chiefly by the power of that sympathy which tends to assimilation with those we love and respect. To an excess of that tendency, opposed by the unyielding temper of my understanding, I trace some of my most severe moral sufferings. Nevertheless, I have cause to rejoice when I consider that since my present convictions have had to struggle for many years against that weakness of my heart,—since they have triumphed over it, not only in the most perfect absence of all acquaintance with any Unitarians, but while I was surrounded by the most devout believers in the divinity of

Christ—the reasons which have moved me cannot have derived any assistance from personal affection and partiality. But to proceed: not long after my strong attachment to many orthodox and highly religious persons had roused and given full sway to my deeply-seated habits of attachment to a *church* (habits which, when it is remembered that from the age of fourteen I belonged to the most compact and best-organized body of clergy which ever existed, must be found quite natural), my reason resumed its operations against the system which I had thus *wilfully* re-embraced; and my mental anxiety, growing every day more intolerable, brought on the most severe aggravation of my long and painful disease that I ever experienced.

I had not yet at that time settled to my entire satisfaction the important point which forms the subject of the following Letters. I had long been convinced that most of the questions which so hopelessly divide the Church of Christ are not essential to Christianity. I knew that the distinction between *essential* and *non-essential* articles of faith must be arbitrary, since there is no certain rule to distinguish them. But I had not fully made the application of the fact—the absence of a rule not subject to rational doubt—nor found, as I did soon after, that the absence of a rule of dogmatic faith is in perfect conformity with the tenour and spirit of the New Testament. As I had not yet obtained this conviction, and was not indifferent about my duty to God, I could not but feel distressed, when, still under a remnant of those early impressions of identity between *saving faith* and *right opinions*, I found my Orthodoxy crumbling to dust, day by day. I may add, with perfect truth, that my distress was increased by my real attachment to the Church of England, from which I feared I should find it necessary to separate myself. Nor is it difficult to explain the source of that attachment.

Abhorrence of the persecuting spirit which made me renounce my native country is, perhaps, the most active sentiment of my heart. It was natural, therefore, that as soon as I became acquainted with the most powerful antagonist which Popery had ever met, I should cling to it with my whole heart. The Church of England was to me what I conceive the *Maltese* knights must have been to a Christian slave who had escaped from the prisons of Algiers into one of the Order's galleys. A long experience must have been necessary, both to myself and the subject of my illustration, to make us perceive that neither of our places of refuge was the dwelling of the full liberty we sought. But having originally examined the Church of England in its unquestionable character of a most powerful opponent of the encroachments of Rome, my eyes were too dazzled to perceive the essential defects of her constitution and the narrowness of her toleration, till the events of the year 1829 disabused me, not without resistance and pain on my part.

The last fact I shall state is, that in my anxiety to avoid a separation from the Church by the deliberate surrender of my mind to my old Unitarian convictions, I took refuge in a modification of the Sabellian theory, and availed myself of the *moral* unity which I believe to exist between God the Father and Christ, joined to the consideration that Christ is called in the New Testament the *Image* of God, and addressed my prayers to God as appearing in that image. I left nothing untried to cultivate and encourage this feeling by devotional means. But such efforts of mere feeling (and I confess with shame their frequency on my part for the sake of what seemed *most religious*) were always vain and fruitless. Sooner or later my reason has not only frustrated, but punished them. In the last-mentioned instance, the *devout* contrivance would not bear examination. Sabellianism is only Unitarianism disguised in words; and as for the worship of an *image* in its absence, the idea is most unsatisfactory. In this state, however, I passed five or six years; but the return to the clear and definite Unitarianism in which I had formerly been, was as easy as it was natural. An almost accidental (if the result had been to make me a Trinitarian, most people would call it *providential*) correspondence with a gentleman (then personally unknown to me, and whom subsequently I have seen but once) who had some years ago resigned his preferment to profess himself a Unitarian, took place during part of last summer and part of the ensuing winter.[*] This was the *occasion* of my becoming

---

[*] The gentleman whose correspondence with me during the last months of my residence in Dublin, at the end of 1834, moved me to declare myself

aware of the flimsiness of the veil which had long somewhat concealed from me the real state of my religious belief. This flimsy veil once torn, I had no difficult questions of theology to examine: they had all been settled before. Whether I was to continue apparently a member of the Establishment, was a point on which I could not hesitate a moment. For the greatest part of more than twenty years, I had employed all my powers in a manner hardly justifiable except on enthusiastic principles, with the object of continuing in the Church. My only excuse for this must be found in the religious habits which I deeply imbibed in youth. I do not absolutely reproach myself for having so long indulged the disinterested sympathies which made me linger in connection with the Church, when my understanding had fully rejected her principal doctrines: at all events, I derive from that fact the satisfaction of being assured that, far from having embraced Unitarianism in haste, the only fault of which I cannot clear myself is that of reluctance and dilatoriness to follow my conviction in its favour.

As the long and close friendship which I have had with many distinguished members of the clergy is generally known, I must add, in justice to them all, that their influence over me has uniformly acted against the settlement of the views I profess. Without exception,

---

a Unitarian, is the Rev. George Armstrong, now a Unitarian minister in Bristol. I had the satisfaction of seeing him once more since the publication of this Preface.—*Note written in March,* 1839.

all and every one of them are, to my knowledge, conscientious believers in the divinity of Christ. It might be supposed that I had discussed with those nearest to me the subjects which so long and so fully have occupied my mind. But it is not so. It may be a fault in me, but I have always disliked *consultation* as a means of deciding questions respecting which all, whatever can be said for either side, is within the reach of every one. Discussion upon such points appears to me the most unlikely method of satisfying oneself. Argumentative discussion on the divinity of Christ is particularly apt to allure the mind into the snares of verbal criticism concerning individual passages. That subject, on the contrary, should be settled by means of the *collective* impression conveyed by the writings of the New Testament; preceded, however, by a careful examination of the preconceived notions by which education has prepared us all to attach the orthodox meaning to certain leading words and phrases of Scripture. This is the great difficulty. We are brought up under the most deliberate *party prejudices*, sanctioned by the most awful spiritual fears. Unless, therefore, our first care is to examine the real worth of those fears, the unassisted reading of the Scriptures must mislead us. To refer a Trinitarian in doubt to the Scriptures *only*, has, indeed, a great air of candour; but if the person thus sent to that supreme but mute authority has been most assiduously taught to understand it only in one sense, and kept in perfect ignorance of all that has and may be said to prove *that* sense erroneous, his mental associations leave him no choice: it is like inviting a man to venture his all upon dice which have been previously cogged, and shaming him, on the score of impartiality, from listening to those who engage to shew him where the trick lies. Nevertheless, in my own case, I solemnly declare that I employed no Unitarian works to counterbalance the prejudices of my education. I never read any defence of Unitarianism, till, in 1818, the study of the New Testament *alone* had made me a Unitarian.

I trust I may still venture to add a few words respecting what I have experienced and observed since I fairly and honestly began to act in full conformity with my conviction. Having never before been in any Dissenting place of worship whatever, and conceiving from what I had heard that the absence of a regular Liturgy in all, and that of real devotion in those of Unitarians, made them quite offensive to persons accustomed to the Church service, I strongly feared I should be obliged to follow Milton's example, and abstain from public worship. Wishing, however, to satisfy myself by personal observation, I went, soon after my arrival in this town of Liverpool, to one of the Unitarian chapels. The effect which the service produced upon me was recorded in my private journal as soon as I returned to my lodgings; but the passage is too long to be inserted here. Suffice it to declare, as I do in the most solemn manner, that I never enjoyed a more devout and sublime impression than I received there. My almost constantly repeated attendance has not weakened the effect of the truly sublime Unitarian worship with which I have become acquainted. I have since attended divine worship in another chapel of the same denomination; and the original impression has been confirmed. Sunday, which, owing to the constant struggle of my mind at church, and the frequent internal rejection of passages in the Liturgy, was formerly to me a day of pain and suffering, is now one of enjoyment. The admirable combination of beautiful hymns with prayers no less beautiful, and a sermon in which I have hitherto never failed to find instruction and support to my religious feelings, all contribute to make me enjoy the service of the Lord's-day. I must add, that I have never joined congregations in which attention and devotion were more visible in all, including the numerous charity children who attend the service. It is a great misfortune that the spirit of Orthodoxy stands like "a great gulf fixed" between Churchmen and Unitarians. Could impartial good men "come and see," though they might remain attached to their opinions, they would be certainly delivered from a multitude of most uncharitable prejudices.

I conclude by protesting against the supposition that the following little work is intended as a defence of Unitarianism. In it I certainly make use of my Unitarian views for argument and illustration; but I do that incidentally, and almost exclusively, in the last Letter. Unitarianism is not in want of any new defence: nor would I waste my time in entering upon a question through which every one may find his way, provided he chooses to examine candidly what is already within the reach of every one: I shall not, therefore, consider myself bound to answer any anti-Unitarian observations which may be directed against me. I do not fear that my declining a controversy, for which my constant ill health particularly unfits me, may injure the cause of Unitarianism. I beg leave to refer any champion of Orthodoxy who may be inclined to stand in defence of the Athanasian doctrine, to try what he can do against the works already in existence. I particularly refer controversial divines to "A VINDICATION OF UNITARIANISM, and SEQUEL," by the Rev. James Yates; and to the recent work of Professor Norton, of Cambridge, U.S., entitled "A STATEMENT OF REASONS FOR NOT BELIEVING THE DOCTRINES OF TRINITARIANS CONCERNING THE NATURE OF GOD AND THE PERSON OF CHRIST."

J. B. W.

Liverpool, June 20, 1835.

HERESY AND ORTHODOXY.

LETTER I.

My dear Friend,

You desire to have a compendious history of Heresy, and of the various means which have been employed by Christians to prevent it. Since, a few years ago, I undertook to write a history of the Inquisition, I have never lost sight of that subject. My daily reading has generally had some reference to it; and there are copious notes among my papers which attest how earnestly I have wished to accomplish the intended work. Were it not a historical task, and, consequently, one which demands research, I believe that, in spite of a broken constitution, I should not have found it (as has hitherto happened) totally above my power. But an old man, nearly confined to his room, cannot by dint of industry and perseverance supply the want of an extensive library of reference; and, as I see no immediate probability of removing this difficulty, I much fear that either my remaining mental activity, or my life, will be at an end before I can write my intended History of the Inquisition.

Yet I am extremely anxious not to drop into my grave without imparting to my fellow-christians what I consider the most important part of the proposed work. I am convinced, that in vain should I accumulate narratives of horrors perpetrated by the various authorities to which we may, collectively, give the name of *Inquisition*, unless I defined the object against which their efforts have been directed. The awful realities of those efforts crowd upon my mind the moment that the name *Inquisition* is uttered; yet one full half of my subject assumes the character of a shadow every time I attempt to place it before me. What is *Heresy?* I well know the sufferings which this word has occasioned to millions of individuals who gloried in the name of Christians. I know that among the sources of bitter anguish which have sprung up in the Christian world, as distinguished from the ancient and from the still unchristianized societies, none can contend with *Heresy*. But when I ask, What is Heresy? I find no one who can give me a satisfactory answer. Can it be, then, that the torrents of tears and blood which have been shed on account of heresy have been occasioned by a phantom, a mental shadow, a mere mist of the mind?

Many, I suspect, will consider this question as totally unconnected with a history of the Inquisition, chiefly intended for the use of Protestants. Among such readers not one can be found ignorant of the meaning of heresy, as punished by that tribunal. "What (it will be said) is this speculative question to *us?* Let us have facts, from which we may derive a clear and vivid idea of the excesses and horrors into which Roman Catholic bigotry is able to betray even sincerely pious men of that communion."

Now, if I could acquiesce in this wish, I should be

attempting a worse than useless work. I cannot add any new horrors to those which, in connection with the Inquisition, both the pen and the graver have already laid before the public. We certainly have reason to be glad that such records have not been lost. But the bare repetition of pictures so shocking and heart-rending is by no means instructive, and may be, in many cases, injurious. While dwelling upon the cruelties of the Inquisitors, such Christians as still consider it a moral duty to oppose heresy by the infliction of some kind and degree of suffering, are apt to exult in their own enlightened Christianity, and feel more and more confident that, by the mere *diminution of punishment*, the act of persecuting religious error may be changed into an act of charity. But be it far from me to cherish such a delusion among Protestants, by casting unnecessary odium upon the Catholics. Yet such must be the effect of a history of the Inquisition which does not begin by settling the notions of *Heresy* and *Orthodoxy*. The Protestant's sympathy for those who have suffered in defence of his own opinions, or rather for opposing those he detests, may easily prove pernicious to both his intellect and heart. Sympathy, when originating in the interests of a cause with which we are identified, may become gross and passionate selfishness. The usual disguise of this perverted feeling is *love of Christian truth*. The generality of Protestants are satisfied when they tell you that they abhor the Church of Rome, because she opposes *Christian truth* by persecution. But these Protestants ought to remember, that it was in defence of *Christian truth* that the Inquisitors lighted up their fires.

I foresee the inevitable result of what I have said. I know that the number of Protestants who will be shocked by this representation of the Inquisition is extremely great. On reading it, the brain of many well-meaning persons will be instantly seized with a feverish confusion, which, if encouraged by circumstances, would lead them to renew the old Smithfield scenes on the man who, calling himself a Protestant, has the boldness to assert that the Inquisition had Christian truth for its object. But let us consider what is that which men understand by *Christian truth* when they accuse others of *heretical error;* in other words, what is *that* which the Catholics have thought it their duty to defend by severe punishments, and many or most of the Protestants by penalties or privations less revolting?

My fancy sets before me the immense variety of expressions by which, when these lines are laid before the public, the countenances of my readers will shew their disapprobation of the question which I have just now proposed. "What! are Christians to be asked by one who professes Christianity, what is meant by Christian truth? Does this writer mean to insinuate that Christian truth has no *real* existence?"

Still, I must insist upon having an answer to my question. For, seeing Christians shedding each others' blood during many centuries, and, even at this day, ready to draw the sword in favour of opposite doctrines to which the various parties, respectively, give the name of *Christian truth*, I have a strong ground to believe that there is some grievous error concealed in those two words. Nor is this at all surprising. The more obvious and plain the leading terms of some questions appear, the greater the danger of their being used by the disputants in various and even opposite senses, without the least suspicion of inaccuracy; for nothing appears more free from obscurity than words of indefinite meaning when they become familiar.

What do divines understand by *Christian truth?* The answer, at first, appears obvious. "Christian truth (it will be said) is what Christ and his apostles knew and taught concerning salvation under the gospel." Thus far we find no difficulty; but (let me ask again) where does this exist as an object *external* to our minds? The answer appears no less obvious than the former: "In the Bible."—Still I must ask, Is the MATERIAL Bible the Christian truth about which Christians dispute? "No (it will be readily said); not the MATERIAL Bible, but the SENSE of the Bible."—Now (I beg to know) is the SENSE of the Bible an object *external* to our minds? Does any *sense* of the Bible, accessible to man, exist anywhere but in the mind of each man who receives it from the words he reads? The Divine Mind certainly knows in what sense those words were used; but as we cannot compare our mental impressions with that model and original of all truth, it is clear that by the *sense* of the Bible we must mean our own sense of its meaning. When, therefore, any man declares his intention to defend *Christian truth,* he only expresses his determination to defend his *own notions,* as produced by the words of the Bible. No other *Christian truth* exists for us in our present state.

I feel confident that what I have now stated is *a fact,* which every reflecting person may ascertain beyond doubt by looking into his own mind: yet I know that few will attempt the mental examination necessary for the acknowledgment of this fact. A storm of feeling will rise at the view of the preceding argument, and impassioned questions, whether Christianity is a dream —whether Christ could leave us in such a state of uncertainty—whether there is no difference between truth and error, with many others more directly pointed at myself, will bring the inquiry to the end of all theological questions—abuse, hatred, and (were it not for the protection, alas! of the great and powerful multitude who, "caring not for these things," take, nevertheless, more interest in the public peace than Gallio) severe bodily suffering, and perhaps death.

The mental *fact* which I have stated is, nevertheless, as unchangeable as the intellectual laws to which God has subjected mankind; as fixed as the means employed by God himself to address his revelation to us. The *Christian truth* which man can make an object of defence, is an impression which exists in his own mind: it is *his own* Christian truth which he wilfully identifies with the Christian truth which is known to the Divine Mind. That each individual is bound to hold that Christian truth which he conscientiously believes to have found; that it is the great moral duty of every man to prepare himself conscientiously for the undisturbed reception of the *impression* which he is to revere and to follow as *Christian truth*, I cannot doubt at all. I acknowledge also the duty of every man to assist others (without intrusion), as much as it may be in his power, in receiving a mental impression similar to that which he venerates as Christian truth. But it is at this point that a fierce contest arises; and the reason is this: certain men wish to force all others to reverence (at least *externally*), not the mental impression, the *sense*, which each receives from the Bible—not the conviction at which each has arrived—but the impression and conviction of some theological sect or church. The Christian truth of some privileged leaders (it is contended by every church respectively) should be recognized as Christian truth by all the world: in more accurate, because more scientific language, Christian parties of the most different characters have for eighteen centuries agreed only in this—that the *subjective* Christian truth of certain men should, by compulsion, be made the *objective* Christian truth to all the world: *i.e.* that the *sense* which the Scriptures did at some time or other convey, or still convey, to such and such men, should be acknowledged as identical with that sense which was in the mind of the writers of the Bible—the true sense which is known to the Divine Mind.

Opposition to these various standards of Christian truth, with those who respectively adopt them, is HERESY.

The question of *Inquisition* or *no Inquisition*, among Christians, is identical with this: Has Christ, or have his apostles, declared that the mental impression of any man or men, in regard to Christian truth, shall be received by all as the only *real* Christian truth?[*]

[*] In a history of the INQUISITION, I would not use that word in any other sense but that of an authority employing means of compulsion in defence of Christianity in general, and of the doctrines considered by some denomination of Christians as exclusively those of Christ and his apostles. But in a work chiefly intended to shew that the spirit of the Roman Catholic Inquisition exists wherever the notion prevails that Orthodoxy and Saving Faith are identical, I think I may be allowed to apply the name of *Inqui-*

That this might have been done, that Christ might have commanded that his followers should pay the same reverence to what some men declared to be Christian truth, as if he himself attested it, is not only conceivable, but appears also, at first sight, a thing antecedently probable: and it is, indeed, this antecedent probability, considered in itself and without due attention to the multitude of facts that contradict it, which is the true basis of POPERY. This very natural delusion is the main foundation of the Church of Rome; this is the obstacle which stopped the progress of the Reformation almost at once; this is the secret power which, at different periods and in various places, seems to make the Reformation recede, and restore the ground to Popery. Protestantism, if established on the basis of ORTHODOXY, *i.e.* the belief of a Rule of Faith different from individual conviction, must be annihilated between UNBELIEF and CATHOLICISM. By this supposition, by lay-

sition to all the means used among Christians to prevent or check that perfect liberty of scriptural interpretation which, in my opinion, and according to *the Protestant principle*, belongs to every disciple of Christ. In this sense it appears to me unquestionable, that, if Christ had established some authority to which individuals should bow, all that class of Christians whose duty in such a case would be to *conform*, must be under some sort of *Inquisition*. Those who conceived themselves charged with the preservation of Orthodoxy would be bound to watch over the opinions of the rest; while all such as had humbly submitted themselves to the appointed authority, would, in conformity with the tendencies of human nature, act as spies against the liberty of their bolder brethren. Is nothing of this kind to be found in this politically free country? Is there no moral *Inquisition* in great Britain and Ireland? Who knows but these Letters may act as a TEST?

"A sprightly academic was one day making some free observations upon the canons before an eminent sage of the law: 'Beware, young man,' says the prudent counsellor of the *holy office*, 'and remember that there are *starving* as well as *burning* Inquisitions.'"—*The Confessional.*

ing this treacherous foundation, Protestantism not only exposes itself to inevitable ruin, but places Christianity defenceless before the host of its opposers. If there must be an external or *objective* rule of faith, besides the words of the Bible; if the mass of Christians must submit to the decisions of another authority, by whatever name it may be described—Pope, Council, Church, Reformers—the Church of Rome can fear no rival. You may raise doubts against its supremacy; you may fill volumes with interpretations and various readings of the writings which attest the early and almost universal recognition of Rome as the centre of Christian unity; but how very few minds, if inclined to that degree of superstition which, in most cases, attends what is called a *pious character*, will not be overpowered by the preeminence of Rome in the Christian world!

"Doubts and objections (the Roman Catholic will say) are inseparable from the most important truths. But, if a judge of controversies is to be acknowledged (as most Protestants confess), what prudent man will hesitate between one so distinguished and eminent as ours, and those whom the Reformation set up? You blame us for grounding our Christian certainty on the *questionable* fact of the divine appointment of Rome to be the head of the Christian world; but can this uncertainty be compared with that which lies at the very foundations of your churches? A few divines meet, and draw up a list of theological propositions; the secular power takes them under its protection; ejects the clergy who will not submit to them; fences the Articles, for a long period, with penalties and civil disabilities, and makes them the rule of Christian faith FOR

EVER.* This is what you call the judgment of the Church, which to oppose is HERESY. It is Heresy now to dissent from the Thirty-nine Articles; but there was (it seems) a happy moment when the notions of a few individuals could be set up, without Heresy, against the judgment of a well-defined and well-constituted church, to which all Christians except HERETICS had for ages submitted their private views on Christianity."

"Settle your disputes (says the unbeliever, on the other hand), and then I will listen to your arguments in defence of Christianity. Both of you, Romanists and Protestants, offer me salvation on condition that I embrace the Christian faith. You offer me a sovereign remedy, which is to preserve me alive in happiness through all eternity; but I hear you accusing each other of recommending to the world, not a remedy but a *poison;* a poison, indeed, which, instead of securing eternal happiness, must add bitterness to eternal punishment. You both agree that it is of the *essence* of Christianity to accept certain doctrines concerning the manner in which the Divine Nature exists; the moral and intellectual condition in which man was created; our present degradation through the misconduct of our

---

* I was not aware how recently and distinctly Parliament had decreed that the faith of the Church of England and Ireland shall remain *for ever* what the former Acts of the Legislature made it. But in No. CXXII. of the *Edinburgh Review,* p. 506, I found the following extract from the Act of Union of England and Ireland. By the fifth article of the Act of Union, it is ruled, "That the Churches of England and Ireland, as now by law established, shall be united into one Protestant Episcopal Church, to be called the United Church of England and Ireland; and the *doctrine, worship, discipline, and government* of the said United Church *shall be, and shall remain in full force* FOR EVER, *as the same are now by law established."*

first parents; the nature of sin, and the impossibility of its being pardoned except by pain inflicted on an innocent person; the existence or non-existence of living representatives of Christ and his apostles; a church which enjoys, collectively, some extraordinary privileges in regard to the visible and the invisible world; the presence of Christ among us by means of transubstantiation, or the denial of such presence: all this, and much more, some of you declare to be contained in, and others to be opposed to, the Scriptures; and even here there is a fierce contention as to whether those Scriptures embrace the whole of that Christianity which is necessary for salvation, or whether tradition is to fill up a certain gap. I am, therefore, at a loss how to account for the invitation you give me. To me (the unbeliever might continue) it is quite evident, that the ablest opponents of Christianity never discovered a more convincing argument against REVELATION in general, than that which inevitably arises from your own statements, and from the controversies of your churches. God (you both agree), pitying mankind, has disregarded the natural laws fixed by himself, and for a space of four thousand years and more has multiplied miracles for the purpose of acquainting men with the means of obtaining salvation, and avoiding eternal death, *eternal death* signifying almost universally, among you, *unending torments*. But when I turn to examine the result of this (as you deem it) *miraculous and all-wise plan,* I find it absolutely incomplete; for the whole Christian world has been eighteen centuries in a perpetual warfare (not without great shedding of blood), because Christians cannot settle what is that faith which alone can save us. Have you not thus demonstrated that the revelation of which you boast cannot be from God? Do you believe, do you wish me to believe, that, when God had decreed to make a *saving truth* known to the world, he failed of that object, or wished to make Revelation a snare?"

That abundance of declamation may be used against this reasoning, no one acquainted with controversial books will doubt; but I cannot conceive how it may be met by a satisfactory answer. If saving faith implies ORTHODOXY, *i.e.* acquiescence in a certain collection of abstract deductions from the Scriptures as logically true, or properly inferred from the language of Scripture, and no higher and more certain means to attain this object have been given by God to men than their individual logical powers; the discovery of saving faith has an infinite number of chances against it, in respect to each individual: to use more definite language, the chance of success in the search after saving faith, is as one to the number of sects and subdivisions of sects which now divide, and may still further subdivide, the Christian world. Could this be the plan of the All-wise and All-good for the salvation of his creatures? Could such a communication be called a REVELATION? What would it have revealed unless it were the melancholy fact, that the lovers of truth among mankind could be rendered still more unsettled, restless, and unhappy, than they were under the reign of pagan philosophy?

"You would, then, make us Papists," will be the indignant retort. If any one becomes a Papist in consequence of my observations, the blame must be divided (though not in equal shares) between those Protestant divines who cherish the true root of Popery in the supposed necessity of *Orthodoxy*, and the delusion of such as can believe that the difficulty against Christianity which arises from that supposition, is avoided by setting up an *infallible church*, without a clear and unquestionable appointment of it by God. The share of blame, however, which must fall to the Protestant divines who allow the snare of Orthodoxy to lie before the feet of the laity, must be by far the greater. Within the reach, as they are, of mental freedom, and surrounded by the results of free inquiry in other branches of knowledge, they ought long since to have been struck by the mass of difficulties which the increase of knowledge accumulates, day after day, against Christianity, when it is identified with any of the scholastic theories which are embodied in the existing CONFESSIONS OF FAITH.*

But no deep study of meditation is required in order to be convinced that the necessity of Orthodoxy for salvation is no part of the gospel of Christ. We need only notice the plain *fact*, that we have no revealed *rule* by which to ascertain, with moral certainty, which doctrines are right and which are wrong. As nothing relating to revelation can be more certainly known than

---

* "We may talk, then, of the sufficiency of the Scriptures as we please ; but while the laws establishing subscription to human formularies remain, the voice of the Articles shall alone be heard: the ignorance and superstition of mankind shall for awhile preserve the shadow of religion in our land, but its substance shall be nowhere found. *Improvements in science and the arts shall at length disclose the astonishing absurdity of our national faith. The Scriptures shall be disbelieved, because their genuine simplicity and excellence are concealed by designing men from human view; the Articles shall be disbelieved, because they are held forth to it.*" Dr. John Jebb, Letters on Subscription, Letter III.

I give the concluding part of the quotation in italics, to call the attention of the reader to the uncontrived coincidence of the passage in the text.

the absence of such a *rule*, it must be evident to all who believe that the gospel is the means appointed by God for our spiritual happiness, that SALVATION cannot depend on ORTHODOXY. The gospel cannot consist in abstract doctrines, about which men of equal abilities, virtue, and sincerity are, and have always been, divided. Once establish this principle, and the objection which, on the supposition of Orthodoxy, irresistibly opposes revelation, is instantly rendered powerless.

"To what, then (it will be asked), is SAVING FAITH reduced if it does not consist in ORTHODOXY, or the belief of right doctrines?"—I answer, to an act which does not depend on the fallible understanding of man, but on his WILL, assisted by the ever-ready grace of God. Since orthodox belief, without a divinely appointed judge to sanction it, is a matter of the greatest uncertainty, it is inconceivable that it should have been made the condition of eternal happiness by a merciful God. Eternal happiness must be independent of the innumerable and inculpable errors and weaknesses of the human understanding, when it employs itself upon things which, by the confession of those who propose them to be believed, are utterly *inconceivable*. The promises of the gospel must have been attached to a MORAL, not to a LOGICAL act. It must be an act in which to fail is blamable; the failure must be, not a *mistake*, but a *sin*. We cannot suppose SAVING FAITH to have its foundation in the understanding, without implying that God has made the chances of men's salvation commensurate with the strength of their intellectual powers, as well as with their opportunities of training those powers, and of assisting them by means of acquired knowledge

—a supposition perfectly untenable: for, putting aside the important consideration, that no moral responsibility can lie on the intellect as *a faculty*, we know, by repeated experience, that men of the highest mental powers are opposed on points which most Christians deem essential. The only consistent theory of saving faith, as depending on doctrines, is that which contends for the existence of a divinely appointed judge. Could that appointment be proved, the acquiescence in the decisions of the infallible judge would be a moral act. Since, therefore, the non-existence of such a judge places us in a dilemma, that either Christianity is an imperfect work, or that saving faith does not consist in Orthodoxy, every sincere believer in the gospel, whose mental courage is not weakened by superstition, must unhesitatingly conclude, that no error on abstract doctrines can be HERESY, in the sense of a wrong belief which endangers the soul.*

Happily the question, whether there exists a divinely appointed judge of Orthodoxy, is one which may be solved without profound learning or a prolonged discussion. The non-existence of a judge divinely appointed to remove doubts, becomes a certainty the moment that the appointment itself is proved to be doubtful. We cannot, without either folly or impiety, suppose that God would attempt to remove one uncertainty by another. The existence of a *divinely* appointed judge of doubtful points is fully disproved the moment that any obscurity appears in the supposed commission.

All Catholics, and most Protestants, will probably unite in the reply, that absolute certainty is inconsistent

* See note at the end.

with our present state of existence. To this I answer, that, in regard to the appointment of any means to remove uncertainty, the All-wise Being could not want resources to produce in us the highest degree of moral confidence of which we are capable. But how short of that point fall the proofs which the Catholics give us of the appointment of their infallible judge! How extremely feeble are the attempts of those Protestants who wish to find a church somewhere, which, though liable to error, is nevertheless to settle our doubts, as if it were infallible! Yet such things are seriously proposed by men of talents and learning! How can we be surprised to find that a great portion of the most intelligent part of the world turns away with pity or disgust from theological writers?

But to return to our principal subject: These lamentable attempts to find a rule of Orthodoxy arise from the false notion, that the union of Christians into a moral body must depend on *unity of doctrine.* And here I wish it to be observed, that, if such unity had been intended by Providence, it might have been attained with the highest degree of moral certainty by means of such an appointment as that which took place in the old dispensation in regard to the Jewish priesthood. Such method of producing unity of doctrine is not only conceivable, but obvious; and, indeed, to none so obvious as to the Founder of Christianity and his immediate disciples, as Jews by birth and education. It is not necessary, in this place, to appeal to the supernatural wisdom of Christ and his apostles. Even men of no uncommon capacity could not, in their circumstances, have overlooked the means employed by Moses to give UNITY to the Jewish theocracy. A solemn consecration of a POPE, and of a certain number of BISHOPS, as distinct from PRIESTS; a formulary for keeping up a legitimate succession, and a few rules for the *external* conditions by which Christians might, at all times, know both whom they were to follow as their infallible guides, and in what circumstances those guides should be considered in a state of supernatural enlightenment, would have reduced the question of Heresy and Orthodoxy to a degree of simplicity fully adapted to the practical purpose of DOCTRINAL UNITY. Since, therefore, the true means of producing and perpetuating that unity were so obvious, and since those supposed to have been appointed have, on the contrary, proved wholly ineffectual, we must inevitably conclude that doctrinal unity was not intended by Christ. To assert that such unity was desired by him, and that he nevertheless overlooked the obvious means by which his object might have been accomplished, is to make him inferior to any man of common penetration. The FAITH, therefore, proclaimed in the New Testament, cannot be ORTHODOXY; the Heresy deprecated in a few places of that collection of writings, cannot be LOGICAL ERROR.*

* That the word heresy was used by St. Paul in the sense of *practical dissension*, can hardly be doubted. The only writer in the New Testament who uses that word besides St. Paul is the author of the 2nd Epistle attributed to Peter, a document whose authenticity is more than suspected by some of the best and most pious critics. In this latter passage alone it seems to mean false doctrine. But as the notion of practical dissension necessarily embraces the notion of opinion (*sensc*, in Latin *placitum*), and it is clear that the divisions and disturbances, which may be expressed by the word dissension, cannot take place without the dissenting parties charging each other with *error*, the two notions have very naturally been mixed up together.

But if ORTHODOXY cannot be the principle of union among Christians, upon what are men to agree in order to belong to the CONVOCATION,* or people of Christ? I believe that the Apostle Paul has said enough to answer this question. When, by using the word *anathema*, he rejects from his spiritual society even an angel from heaven, were it possible that such a being should " preach another gospel," he lays down the only principle, without which there can be no communion among Christians. Unhappily the word GOSPEL, like the word Faith, is constantly understood as expressing a certain number of dogmatical articles. Owing to this perversion of the original meaning, these very passages of Paul are conceived to support the long-established notion that Orthodoxy is the only condition of Christian communion; and want of it, a sufficient cause for *anathema*. I have, however, already proved, that Orthodoxy, without a supreme judge of religious opinions, is a phantom; and since it is demonstrable that no such judge has been appointed, it clearly follows that the Apostle Paul, by the name of *gospel*, could not mean a string of dogmatic assertions. It is necessary, therefore, to ascend to the original signification of the word gospel, if we are not to misunderstand the reason of the anathema pronounced

---

* It is very difficult to discard from the mind the wrong associations which the English word CHURCH attaches to the notion expressed by the original word ἐκκλησία, in Latin *ecclesia*. If *church*, as some etymologists believe, comes from a Teutonic root (kirk) of the same signification as the Latin *circus* and the English *circle*, its signification might originally have been similar to that of *ecclesia*, in consequence of the same mental process which made *corona*, a crown, a *ring*, express a collected multitude; *vulgi stante corona;* but nothing is more remote from the ideas raised in the mind by the word *church*, than this. *Convocation* seems to approach the nearest to the original signification of *ecclesia*.

by Paul. Let such as wish to rise above the clouds of theological prejudice, remember that the whole mystery of godliness is described by the expression of "glad tidings." *Sad*, not glad tidings, indeed, would have been the apostles' preaching, if they had announced a salvation depending on *Orthodoxy*, for (as I have said before) it would have been salvation depending on chance. But salvation, promised on condition of a change of mind from the love of sin to the love of God (which is *repentance*); on a surrender of the individual will to the will of God, according to the view of that divine will which is obtained by trust in Christ's example and teaching, which is *faith*; a pardon of sins independent of harassing religious practices, sacrifices, and ascetic privations—these were "glad tidings of great joy," indeed, to all who, caring for their souls, felt bewildered between atheism and superstition.*

As this gospel was, and must always be, the very essence of Christianity, to deny it, or (what amounts to the same) to substitute another in its place, must, for ever, be contradictory of the denomination CHRISTIAN. Now it is well known that those who had deceived Paul's Galatian converts taught the necessity of circumcision for *that* salvation which the gospel promised to repentance. Nothing, therefore, could be more natural, nothing more directly flowing from the commission he had received, than to declare his abhorrence of those who practically abolished the very gospel which it was

* "Thus it is written, and thus it behoved Christ to suffer, and to rise from the dead the third day: and *that repentance and remission of sins should be preached in his name among all nations.*"—Luke xxiv. 46, 47. This is the commission given to the apostles by Jesus himself.

the dearest object of his life to spread. The gospel, in fact, being one single announcement, warranted by Christ, namely, remission of sins upon repentance, and eternal life to those who embrace these "glad tidings;" to promise these same things on any other condition is an endeavour to render the true gospel useless to mankind.

Similar to this is the principle which the Apostle John applies to some of the Gnostics. Paul pronounces anathema on any one who should preach another gospel, which, as he declares, "is not another," *i.e.* is no gospel, no glad tidings at all.* John, proceeding on the same principle, applied the name of ANTICHRIST to any one who denies that Jesus is the Christ. It is, besides, of importance for the right understanding of some such expressions of St. John, to know that, of the Gnostics, who, from the notion of the natural impurity of all matter, denied that the Messiah had a body, a considerable number embraced also the practical error, that it was the duty of those who aspired to perfection to give up the body to all kinds of impurity, out of contempt for the evil principle, the author (as they believed) of the material part of the universe. That even the common civilities of life should not be interchanged by Christians with such practical Antinomians, is perfectly consistent with a total absence of orthodox intolerance.†

Such as I have just described it, was the UNITY OF THE FAITH among the truly apostolic Christians. Let

---

* It is hardly necessary to observe that, by saying "which is not another," Paul intended to say, which is not a gospel. He could certainly not mean that it was the *same*.

† See note at the end.

us never forget that FAITH means TRUST, and we shall readily perceive that the unity of trust, in regard to spiritual safety, must have been UNITY OF FAITH. The acceptance, therefore, of the "good tidings," namely, remission of sins upon repentance, and eternal life by trust in Christ as the moral KING promised to the Jews, to deliver them from the condemnation of the law, and to the Gentiles, as their "light" and their "Saviour," who was to rescue them from vice and the darkness of idolatry, the acceptance of this gospel was all that the apostles and their assistant messengers of salvation demanded. But as this belief was a living principle, bearing in itself that peculiar spirit or influence which Christ had promised to his sincere followers,* it would naturally extend its activity to all the mental faculties, and make them converge their powers to that centre of the soul's new life. Studies of all kinds, especially the study of the Scriptures, would be carried on within the powerful attraction of the great truth,—Jesus of Nazareth is the Son of God, the Saviour or great benefactor of mankind: happiness, here and hereafter, depends upon trust in his promises, and faithfulness to his precepts. When, therefore, a point of contact between the one essential principle of Christianity, and any other result of reflection or experience, offered itself to view, it would be greedily seized for the purpose of confirming or illustrating that principle. Some of these views would have a real foundation in the one original truth of Christianity; some would be plausible or fanciful

---

* This is true in a MORAL sense. The notion of a physical, yet supernatural SPIRIT, I had already discarded when I published this book. See note at the end. (*Note written in October*, 1837.)

deductions, but harmless; others would be false, and perhaps *dangerous*, to that great truth, if followed up too closely and too logically. Yet all this was deemed consistent with the profession of real Christianity. Such is, indeed, Paul's view of the subject, as any one will find who shall study with an unprejudiced mind the third chapter of his first Epistle to the Corinthians.

No one acquainted with that scriptural document will deny that "the envying, strife, and divisions"—the HERESIES, in the scriptural sense of the word—which agitated the Christian society at Corinth, had their source in the peculiarities of the additional doctrines by which different teachers wished to distinguish themselves. It follows, therefore, that Paul had such doctrines in view, while he was earnestly urging his Corinthian "children in Christ" to put aside these sources of discord. Let us now attentively consider the manner in which Paul treats these differences of DOCTRINE. He certainly does not (as subsequent theologians) appeal to some supreme tribunal in the church; he does not urge his own inspiration, and the consequent duty of taking his words as divine oracles on all occasions; he does not (as many at present would expect) claim to himself the right and authority of stopping the mouth of those teachers. His words throw the clearest light on my subject. I insert them, with such transient paraphrases as, I trust, the context will support. I only beg you not to forget that the point which the apostle had to settle was, the practical question of *variety of doctrine* in the church of Corinth.

"According to the grace of God which is given to me (he says) as a wise master-builder, I have laid the foundation, and another buildeth thereon. But let every man take heed how he buildeth thereupon; for other foundation can no man lay than that is laid, which is Jesus Christ. Now if any man (St. Paul proceeds) build upon this foundation gold, silver, precious stones, wood, hay, stubble, every man's work shall be made manifest; for the day (*i.e. time*) shall declare it; because it (the work thus done by men) shall be revealed by fire (by close and searching examination, arising from the vehement contests of Christians), and the fire shall try every man's work of what sort it is. If any man's work abide, which he hath built thereupon, he shall receive a reward (in the assistance he shall have given to the gospel, and in God's approbation: secondary views in conformity with the foundation will stand). If any man's work shall be burned, he shall suffer loss (additional doctrines, which must perish like stubble and wood by fire, will be a loss, a fine or penalty, to the injudicious preacher); but he himself (if he has not given up the foundation, Jesus Christ, or betrayed it for another) will be saved (will be acquitted notwithstanding his errors), yet so as by fire" (with difficulty and the loss of his labour).*

If such be the true meaning of this, to many obscure,

---

* I had originally followed what I believe is the general notion, that, by *fire*, the apostle meant persecution. But taking for my guide the clear assertion that TIME would be the great instrument in removing the false notions which philosophical teachers were then mixing with the foundation of the gospel, I feel pretty certain that the *fire*, which is figuratively added as the more proximate instrument of the separation, must have an analogy to *time* in regard to the predicted effect. But if *time* can bring about the separation of *error* which has been mixed up with *truth*, it is because it allows sufficient space for discussion and the struggle of contending views. *Persecution* (which is the common signification given to *fire*) could not produce that effect; on the contrary, it generally confirms the errors of the persecuted.

to others delusive, passage (and I believe the interpretation here given cannot easily be shaken), the question of Orthodoxy, with all its practical difficulties, is at an end. And here let me observe, that the coincidence of my preceding argument with this remarkable passage was not at all prepared by my taking a clue from the passage itself. The inquiry which I have been pursuing began by the examination of a negative fact—a kind which is ascertained with more certainty than the POSITIVE. I searched for the appointment of a judge of ORTHODOXY. A direct and definite appointment was not found; and this is enough to establish that NEGATIVE FACT beyond doubt. This step enabled me to conclude that ORTHODOXY and SAVING FAITH must be two different things; else the salvation of sincere men would have been made to depend on means attended with the greatest uncertainty. As a well-grounded conviction of the truth of Christianity did not permit me, from this seeming deficiency in its plan, to conclude against the divine origin of the gospel, I proceeded to examine what is left, after excluding all those theological questions on which the most learned as well as most pious persons are divided; all questions, I mean, which cannot be settled without a judge of orthodoxy; and I found this—belief or trust in THE CHRIST, the moral king and instructor of mankind. This is the only point (besides practical precepts) which admits of no doubt among those who receive the testimony of the New Testament: this is the only preaching of Christ's immediate disciples which requires no unerring interpreter. I concluded, therefore, that this belief, this acceptance of the Christ as a moral Lord and Master, is the only condition of being a CHRISTIAN. I was led besides, by numerous considerations, to the persuasion, that other views, more or less connected with this surrender of the individual *will* to the *will* of God, as we know it through the teaching and example of Christ himself—that conjectures about the nature of the Christ himself, and respecting the manner of the Divine existence—that notions relating to our future state, and theories innumerable on the world of spirits and our relations with it—would at all times, but especially immediately after the publication of the gospel, when the human mind was full of the most visionary systems of philosophy, attach themselves to the great and fundamental truth of Christianity. Considering, however, that the gospel might co-exist with errors which did not directly oppose its influence on the will of man (else the gospel could not have been preached till mankind had been completely enlightened by philosophy and science), I felt no doubt that it was the intention of Providence that *secondary* or *collateral* religious views should have free course among Christians, leaving such views to the operation of time, which would finally discover their proper value. Having gone through this mental process, it occurred to me, that, without at all intending it, or having previously thought of the above passage of St. Paul, I had said in other words exactly what the apostle had stated in expressions and metaphors not so familiar to our minds. I had, indeed, frequently dwelt upon that passage; but its meaning remained always enveloped in a mist, till, as it were, by the innate attraction of truth to truth, the result of my thoughts on Orthodoxy and these remarkable words of Paul ran, like two kindred drops, into each other, forming in my mind a clear, full, and definite notion. This cannot be the effect of chance.

LETTER II.

ON HERESY AND ORTHODOXY.

MY DEAR FRIEND,

NOTHING weighs so heavily upon my mind, when engaged on theological subjects, as the constant fear of being misunderstood, and the habitual conviction that no care on my part can possibly avert that danger. A most distinguished writer on the theory of morals (Sir James Mackintosh) complains in a striking manner of the almost insuperable difficulty which popular language presents to the philosopher who undertakes to throw light on the subject of man considered as a moral, responsible, and improvable agent. Yet that obstacle, in philosophy, appears reduced to the dimensions of a molehill, when compared with the mountain which the popular language of theology, and the prejudices inseparably connected with it, cast up in the way of any man who, in the examination of Christianity, ventures to leave the beaten path of scholasticism. The most important words of the New Testament have not only received an indelible false stamp from the hands of the old schoolmen, but those words having, since the Reformation, become common property in the language of the country, are, as it were, thickly incrusted with the most vague, incorrect, and vulgar notions. Thus the word *faith* (for instance), which, at the hands of the Romanist divines, had been nearly deprived of its original meaning, *trust*, which is directly and most exclusively conveyed by πίστις, is still further perverted, by common usage among Protestants, to signify an enthusiastic ardour in asserting what they can neither prove nor express to themselves in definite terms. The faith preached by the Roman Catholics as the only way to salvation, is an act of mental obedience to the Catholic Church, that infallible judge which they suppose to exist somewhere. The faith of many Protestants is an act of passionate asseveration grounded only upon the feelings of each individual, and rendered unalterable by the stubbornness with which they close their eyes, that they may not see any reason to waver.

Now, under such circumstances, can misunderstanding be avoided? The investigation of truth, as in *theory* it is universally acknowledged, demands perfect composure of mind, and the absence of all disturbing passions. But is it possible for a writer who does not flatter popular notions in divinity, to obtain many readers in that state of mind? Can a man who calls upon people, urging their duty to examine their religious notions, and to take the necessary trouble for separating truth from error, avoid giving offence? No. The strongest tendency of the human mind, in respect to religion, is to save itself trouble, either by embracing a superstitious and indiscriminate system of belief, or by dismissing the subject as totally unworthy of attention. Nearly hopeless, however, as this latter state of mind must appear to the theological writer, it is in reality preferable to that of the impassioned believer. The most frequent cause of unbelief, which I have observed in this country, is *disgust*; produced, on the one hand, by misrepresentations of Christianity which defy reason and common sense; and, on the other, by a morbid enthusiasm, which may be, and frequently is, combined with the ambition and selfishness of minds of the lowest description. Now, if a theological writer succeeds in removing from himself the suspicion of his belonging to either of those classes, there are honest and upright men who, in spite of their prejudices against Christianity, will listen to him with temper and candour. Not so the impassioned believer: in his case, the great difficulty is to prevent him from taking his own hasty inferences for your statements. The direct opposite of the proposition which you wish to modify and explain, is instantly assumed as your meaning. If you endeavour, for instance, to ascertain with any degree of precision the notion of INSPIRATION, you are, without appeal, reckoned among those who consider the sacred writers as men of the common stamp, which belonged to their original station in life. If you venture to suggest the probability of some one interpolation in the Bible, you are no longer believed when you assert the general and substantial genuineness of the whole. I cannot but fear, therefore, that in consequence of what I have said respecting the simple condition demanded by the apostles for admission into the society of Christians, I shall be accused of having reduced the gospel to an empty name. But whatever may be the injustice of others towards me, I feel assured that you, at all events, will candidly hear me to the end; allowing me, besides, to endeavour, by insisting upon the arguments already adduced, to set them in a clearer light, and thus prevent, as much as I am able, the misunderstandings which, more for the sake of Christian truth than for my own, I confess that I greatly dread. I shall, therefore, say a few words of explanation relative to that part of my former letter where I spoke of the original terms of admission into the church. I shall, in the next place, add some other considerations which confirm my view: but I must previously remind you of the nature of the argument contained in that letter.

You must have frequently observed the hopelessness of the attempts which are constantly made to establish various points of Christian doctrine by *logical* arguments founded on detached texts of Scripture. You must have seen regular collections of passages, selected with the utmost patience, and arranged into classes with great ingenuity. Of this kind of theological works I do not remember any one more complete than that by which Dr. Samuel Clarke wished to prove his notions of the Trinity. But similar instances are not unfrequent: in fact, most works on controversial divinity are attempts of the same kind to draw some abstract proposition as the unquestionable result of the various expressions of Scripture upon the given subject. You cannot but have observed, moreover, how short all such attempts fall of the intended object; how very seldom any one is convinced by such works, unless, by a predisposition of the will, he reads them in order fully to become or to continue of the same opinion.

I do not mean (and here is an instance of the constant call for explanation) that the Scriptures, especially those of the New Testament, are incapable of conveying a clear and definite sense upon any subject. My observations are confined to the metaphysical points upon which the most pious and most learned Christians are divided; those points, in fact, which relate to the nature and modes of existence of the Deity, the supposed multiplicity of his personality, and the laws according to which he operates upon the human soul, and its principal faculties, intellect, and will. In order that I may protect myself against the cavils to which an imperfect enumeration of such subjects might expose me, I need only say, that I speak of the topics directly connected with these letters; those, namely, upon which the Christian world is divided into ORTHODOX and HETERODOX. Upon such notions of God and his moral character which are both *conceivable* by man and morally useful to him; upon our relations to our heavenly Father, and to his Son, his great messenger; upon our mutual duties in this state of discipline, the New Testament is clear. The proof of that clearness is found in the agreement of Christians in all times and places. The ravings of enthusiasm, and the systematic profligacy of a certain kind of hypocrites, who now and then have ventured to question the sense of the Scriptures on such subjects, do no more prove their obscurity, than the existence of a few human monsters proves an uncertainty in the first moral dictates of our conscience. Absolute certainty, certainty which the passions may not obscure, cannot exist where the will is concerned.

Now, my argument against the necessity of Orthodoxy, *i.e.* the necessity of taking the right side (as it is known to God) on any one of the points of doctrine which divide the Christian world, depends entirely upon the unquestionable fact, that whichever view we choose, there are arguments in favour of the other strong enough to convince men most able to investigate, and most desirous to find the truth. I must not, however, be understood to assert that, in my opinion, the probability on both sides of all such questions is equal. Speaking for myself, I must declare that the evidence in favour of excluding such theories as that of the Trinity in Unity, on the ground that they form no part of the New Testament, is sufficient to produce moral certainty. But I grant—from my own experience at one period of my life, that, under certain habits of mind, produced by the usual catechetical and scholastic instruction, and assisted by that deep-seated and almost general persuasion that all spiritual danger lies on the side of believing what is plain, and all the advantages on the side of asserting what is unintelligible and repugnant to reason—I grant that even the Athanasian Creed may appear as an essential part of the Christian doctrine. Having stated the case of Orthodoxy and Heterodoxy in a manner which gives every possible advantage to those who call themselves exclusively Orthodox, I only wish you to place the fact laid before you in juxtaposition with the intent and purpose of the Christian revelation: I require nothing more for my argument.

If saving faith and acceptance of one particular side of the questions agitated between the divines of various Christian denominations are identical things, the means of salvation must be as uncertain as the chance of choosing the right side of those questions. Here we are placed in the dilemma of creating for ourselves some such rule of Orthodoxy as that of the Roman Catholics

—a process which removes doubt only one step, and ultimately increases it;* or rejecting Christianity as an imperfect and partial system. What man, therefore, who is thoroughly convinced of the truth of the gospel, will not instantly see the plain and only way out of this difficulty—*i.e.* the rejection of the gratuitous hypothesis of Orthodoxy? This *negative* argument, the proof which arises from the total *absence* of an authority sufficient to remove the uncertainty (such as I have explained it) in which the Scriptures leave the disputed points, is of a nature to satisfy any unprejudiced mind, provided it is not in thraldom to superstitious fear. It is not like *positive* proofs derived from various texts, where one expression modifies another, where one metaphor must be brought into agreement with another metaphor, and the reading of one manuscript must be staked against other readings. Here the whole question depends upon the *absence* of some rule, not exposed to *uncertainty*, by which the uncertainty in the sense of the Scriptures, experienced by multitudes of Christians, may be entirely removed. *Probability* is of no avail. If the proposed method of removing *uncertainty* may be reasonably questioned; if the *authority* which claims the right of decision cannot shew a divine appointment, clear, positive, distinct in every respect, it only increases the evil which it was intended to remedy; for it adds a fresh difficulty to those which, on the supposition of the necessity of Orthodoxy, stand, like an impenetrable phalanx, at the very entrance of the way of salvation. Hence the inevitable conclusion, that to be right upon any of

* Less hard 'tis not to err ourselves, than know
If our forefathers erred or no.   COWLEY.

the points so long disputed among Christians cannot be a necessary condition of saving faith; else God would have demanded from us what he evidently has not given us the means to attain. And let it not be forgotten, that the distinction between ESSENTIALS and NON-ESSENTIALS is perfectly arbitrary, and does not remove the difficulty: for by what certain rule can we divide the disputed doctrines into those two classes? I repeat it with the most heartfelt confidence: a just and merciful God, when making the greatest display of his love to mankind, by allowing his beloved Son to die in confirmation of his divine mission, and for the purpose of endearing to us himself, and his proclamation of peace with God by repentance—God, the author and fountain of the blessings prepared for all mankind in his gospel, must not be supposed to have made them dependent on doctrines so intricate, so incapable of being proposed in clear and uncontradictory language, so entirely unconnected with the sources of moral certainty. How could the Father of mercies have bound up the benefits of Christianity within the complicated folds of Orthodoxy, and denied us a clue to solve those riddles? It is almost childish to answer, that we have the Scriptures for that purpose; for, owing to that very notion of Orthodoxy, the Scriptures themselves are, upon those points, the riddle.

Upon this immovable foundation I established the conclusion, that the only indispensable condition of being in the *way of salvation* through the gospel, must be that which remains after the removal of all the doctrines which have been constantly disputed between the Orthodox and the Heterodox. And what can that be?

Exactly that which we find proposed by the apostles: *repent and believe in* the Lord Jesus Christ; *i.e.* change the habitual direction of your *will* from sin to holiness, and TRUST the Lord Jesus Christ as your guide to spiritual safety, as your surety for the hope of eternal happiness.*

If, retorting my own argument, it should be said that questions may also be raised upon the meaning of these words, I shall request the objector to mark this important difference between such *possible* cavil and the prominent difficulties of Orthodoxy. This call of the gospel is addressed to the WILL of every individual, under the direction of his CONSCIENCE. The conscience itself may indeed be perverted by the will, and the result may be (as we know to our sorrow) a rejection of God's merciful invitation. But this is of the very essence of all offers made to a moral agent *as such;* moral agency cannot exist without the power of doing what is morally wrong. RIGHT and WRONG, however, in such matters do not depend on anything *external* to man, but on the object and direction of his WILL. Between this choice and that of *propositions* which fall under the *intellectual judgment*, there is an immense difference. The means which alone can enable the judgment to be right in asserting or denying one thing or another, are not within us. We must search abroad in the universe, and, after the most anxious inquiry, may be unable to give a judgment which is not opposed by *reality*. When the judgment relates to the interpretation of words (which is invariably the case in all questions on the sense of Scripture), the search is still more difficult

* See Note.

In matters of experience we frequently have the object of our examination at hand; but in respect to the sense which the authors of the sacred books wished to convey, it is clear that the only *fact* on which our right judgment depends—the connection of the writer's ideas with his expressions—is entirely out of our reach. All therefore that remains is conjecture. We are obliged to take that for the sense of the writer which, when we have endeavoured to the best of our power to impress our minds with the character, purpose, and peculiar style of the person whose writings we have before us, appears to us most *likely* to have been his meaning. But in regard to moral good and evil, the rectitude of the conscience does not depend on anything external to the *individual*— that domain over which it reigns by the appointment of the Supreme Intelligence, whose representative it is. To the *individual*, the voice of his conscience is the voice of God, and there is no appeal from its decision to a higher tribunal. The great duty of the WILL is to obey it; and the highest degree of perfection at which the WILL can arrive is a state of settled independence from all other powers and influences. It is very true that the moral perceptions, the moral sense, or moral *taste* (as it might well be called) of the conscience, is susceptible of many degrees of quickness and perfection; and, indeed, the moral government of God, as far as we know it, is only a method of training the conscience, and, by means of the conscience, the will of man. For this great purpose, no trial or discipline is of a higher and more powerful nature than the offer of the gospel. When men are called upon to repent, or change their will from the indulgence of the selfish passions to the habitual determination of embracing that which, on every occasion, the conscience shall approve as BEST, they cannot answer with any show of reason that they are not able to understand what is proposed to them. There is no hardship or injustice in proposing to men that they renounce a vicious life, because the abstract notions of vice and virtue are primitive, and not only do not require, but do not admit of explanation. The man who *really* and *truly* wishes to be virtuous, is already in the possession of virtue—is JUSTIFIED from that moment. There is nothing like this in regard to abstract and *objective* Truth: the most ardent wish to attain it, is no pledge of our possessing it. Thus it is that Christianity, unadulterated Christianity, is found in perfect harmony with the nature of our moral being. And observe how the announcement which exclusively constitutes the gospel, contains not only the simple and infallible method of being *justified*, or becoming virtuous, but also that of improving that incipient moral state, and carrying it to the utmost degree of perfection of which human infirmity is capable, under the peculiar circumstances of each individual. The natural question, How am I to proceed, and what am I to expect when I have given up the pursuit of selfish gratification? is answered by means of the doctrines and character of Jesus, as both are known by the report of his life, which is already spread over a great part of the world, and which (were it unobstructed by the theories of Orthodoxy) would soon cover the earth as the waters cover the sea. In the Christ we have a model of human virtue which every conscience, under the *indispensable preparation of repentance* (exactly in the order of things which the gospel proposes), must approve, and which every WILL, subject to conscience, must embrace. How can this gospel be said to lie under doubts and difficulties similar in the slightest degree to those of the Orthodox doctrines? With what colour of reason can this heavenly call upon mankind be compared with the theological requisition to believe abstract statements concerning a person with two natures, and a nature with three personalities, which still remains *one* God? a guilt incurred by proxy, and a justification or state of virtue by a similar substitution? Offer the true gospel, present the moral image of the Christ to the ignorant, or even to savages, in whom the seeds of morality are beginning to be developed, and you will find hearts eager to receive him; but go through the world with your Orthodox creeds in hand, and the intelligent among the uneducated classes will stare, and the educated will turn away with disdain. It is in vain to expect a diffusion of the gospel, approaching in any degree to what the Scriptures would make us expect, so long as missionaries imbued with the essential importance of the Orthodox doctrines attempt the work of announcing Jesus to the heathen. The only missionaries who seem to make a real progress are the Moravians, who, though still burdened with the Confession of Augsburg in their formularies, appear to perceive the necessity of laying it aside while they publish the message of salvation.

Strong, however, as my expressions may seem, I do not intend to blame the numerous and highly respectable class of Christians who, having had the prejudices of Orthodoxy not only transmitted to them by inheritance, but inculcated also by a laborious process of education, and bound up with every public and personal interest of their lives, stand up for that system with all the zeal which Christianity itself would rightly demand. I entreat them, however, to consider how perfectly inconsistent it is with the essential principle of Protestantism to assume a superiority over others in respect to the interpretation of Scripture. If any one is convinced that the Athanasian Trinity is proclaimed in the Bible, let him teach and expound it to the utmost of his power; but let him claim no dominion over the faith of others, and much less assume the power of excommunicating, and denying the name of Christian to any one who receives the Christ as his Lord and Master. Let him remember that the instruction contained in the New Testament has not been addressed to some particular Christians in order that they may expound, digest, and distribute it, in a modified state, to others: the Scripture is addressed to all, without distinction.

Dark inuendoes are heard every day relative to a supposed responsibility of the understanding. Such assertions are, however, thrown out devoid of all proof, and, indeed, are totally incapable of any. As well might people declaim on the responsibility of the eyes, and the moral duty of seeing certain figures and colours in certain places, though the visual organ, straining itself to blindness, should see nothing but vacuity in that direction, or objects perfectly different from those which the moral optician was describing as perfectly visible.*

* Who that once has heard the anecdote of the HOLY HAIR, can avoid being reminded of it in connection with this topic? Among the most valuable relics of an ancient monastery was one of the identical hairs which the Roman soldiers had torn from the head of Christ. This hair

It cannot be too often repeated, that the only responsible part of man is his WILL. The will is, indeed, liable to blame for neglecting or misusing the external as well as the internal means of right perception; but it is perfectly unreasonable to make it answerable for the *perceptions* themselves. It would be *real*, not theological blasphemy (which generally means evil speaking of theological opinions), to say that God would doom any of his rational creatures to eternal misery because, though he had tried, he could not understand the plain demonstration of the truth, that the three angles of any triangle are equal to two right ones. Yet to perceive that truth seems to be in the power even of the most moderate understanding. What then should we say of the assertion, that God dooms to everlasting perdition every one whose reason rejects the Athanasian Creed? Reason itself, that highest faculty of the human soul, whose inalienable privilege is to decide between right

---

was shewn to the public on a certain festival. The devout people looked through a glass into a golden box where the hair *should* be seen. But when the existence of such things is once fully established by faith, the keepers of the treasure take no further pains to facilitate the belief. To place a hair, or even a whole lock, in the box was not difficult. It happened, however, that for many years the box had contained no such thing. A rather too curious and prying Christian, having deposited his oblation of money on the salver that lay upon the table, behind which a priest in his stole was shewing the relic, kept his eye close to the glass for a considerable time. "I can see no hair, father" (whispered he in the ear of the monk).—"No wonder, my son (answered the priest in the same tone of voice), for I have shewn it these twenty years, and have never been able to see it." How many who shew the wonders of Orthodoxy might truly give a similar answer! Yet it is most probable that if the monk and the devotee's dialogue had been overheard, both would have been sent to the Inquisition, to be punished for their visual weakness, and to learn to see better in future.

and wrong, truth and deception, is, not the subject, but the fountain of all moral duty. The WILL alone has duties to perform. One of them is to employ the UNDERSTANDING (the faculty that prepares the information required for the decision of reason) under a habitual love of divine truth, *i.e.* of the correspondence of our conceptions with the existences of God's material and spiritual universe. It is the moral duty of the WILL to use the understanding as a MIRROR,* courting in every direction, and by every means in man's power, the rays of divine truth; and endeavouring, by industry, disinterestedness, and sincerity, to remove the soiling breath of the passions and desires, which so frequently distort those rays, and make them diverge from the mind.

But, above all, the great moral duty of the will, in relation to the conclusions of reason, is VERACITY. The impressions which every individual receives, the reflected truths which, after proper examination, are found to be permanent on the mind, should be sacred to VERACITY. I need not add that this duty is peculiarly incumbent on the Christian respecting the religious truths which he finds in the Scriptures. But excuse me if I repeat, that, in order to prepare ourselves for the performance of this duty, we should remove from the mind every superstitious fear, which, when existing there, must prevent those writings from conveying an unperverted sense. We hear loud and incessant declamations against the pride and presumption which are

---

* "For now we see as by means of a mirror, in hints." This translation seems to me to remove the obscurity which the established version leaves on this interesting passage.—1 *Cor.* xiii. 12.

believed to interfere whenever any one rejects the interpretations of the Orthodox party. But what passion can be compared with the servile fear of many Christians as to its power of paralyzing the intellectual faculties, and preventing the exercise of a manly judgment? Can a trembling soul which sees the gulf of destruction gaping before it during the examination of some contested point; can any one who from the cradle has been made to see every danger on the side of believing what is plain, rational, and consistent, and all imaginable safety in embracing what is most repugnant to common sense and the first laws of reason; can a mind in this state of weakness and trepidation avoid the temptation to close its eyes against the truth, and "speak wickedly for God and talk deceitful for Him"? It would be, indeed, not only useless, but in many cases cruel, to urge any powerful considerations which might disturb the helpless slaves, or rather victims, of an education essentially intolerant; but every man who has courage to think, and loves truth more than he fears obloquy and insult, is bound to caution all those who, possessing a mental character of the same stamp, may not yet be aware of its value, against the dangers which threaten if it be not fully developed. It is to such persons that I address my warnings: let them beware of superstitious fear in the investigation of religious truth; let them encourage in their souls a habitual attention to the duty of VERACITY, and read the Scriptures with a firm determination of not deceiving themselves, for the sake of a false internal peace with early prejudices; and, still more, of not concealing from others whatever impressions may have assumed a clear and prominent character during the examination of the sacred writings. Since *subjective religious truth*, i.e. the impressions which the Scriptures leave on each individual, have not been made by God a matter of OBEDIENCE to any authorized judge of truth; since the meaning of the Scriptures has been left unlimited by the judgment of any external authority; it must be supposed that it is the intention of Providence that the Scriptures be studied, *in common*, by all those who acknowledge their authority; and, if such be the purpose of the Divine Mind, it must be a duty of all Christians not to deceive each other as to the results of their respective perceptions of the sense of the Scriptures. To act otherwise, must be a sin of FALSEHOOD: it must be "holding the truth in unrighteousness" (or translating more literally, "in *injustice;*" for what injustice can exceed that which is done to mankind when any one casts into the common treasury of intellectual experience, as his own TRUTH, as the real impression on his mind, that which is entirely unlike that impression? Such a deliberate LIE, in relation to the Scriptures, must be hateful in the eyes of God. He knows our weakness of judgment, and our consequent liability to error; but what can plead our excuse before Him when we wilfully corrupt and deface the only unquestionable TRUTH we possess—the *reality of our consciousness?* It cannot be our duty to be right in our interpretation of the Scriptures, because God has not given us the means to understand them with moral certainty, except as to their general and practical objects; but we are bound to be VERACIOUS, to state candidly what we see, because in regard to this we are fully conscious whether we speak the TRUTH or a LIE.

From faithfulness to the duty of VERACITY, the Christian world might finally derive the inestimable advantage of knowing what is the most general, most distinct, and most lasting impression made by the Scriptures on the *collective* intellect of those to whom they are *collectively* addressed. That impression, if gathered from the free and unbiassed examination of the most intelligent portion of the Christian world, might properly be called the *natural* sense of the Scriptures. In what department of knowledge do we see, or could a civilized nation endure, the method which is followed in regard to religion? I have, indeed, heard and read of some attempts to perpetuate, by means of oaths, some particular theory of medicine, which at some time or other was considered to have arrived at a perfection above all possibility of improvement. I am aware that the pupils of the school of Hippocrates vowed to the gods never to perform or recommend the operation of lithotomy; and I recollect to have seen, many years ago, in a book written against the use of the Jesuits' Bark, a sentence of excommunication which a high ecclesiastical authority (I have an idea that it was the Pope) had fulminated against any practitioner of medicine that prescribed it. Similar attempts to stop the progress of knowledge, just at the point where the stoppage suited the vanity, the indolence, and interest of some powerful body of men, have been frequent; but they have been gradually swept off by the progress of civilization. Yet the same method of keeping down all Christians to the measure of a certain standard, continues to this day in the fullest vigour. The physician who, in order to please some great and powerful association of medical men, should be found reporting cases contrary to the *impression* of his mind, would justly be ranked with the lowest and most odious individuals of our species. He who, upon receiving his medical diploma, should solemnly engage never to depart from a curative system upon which the professors of the faculty had been fiercely contending for many ages, would be said to betray the interests of humanity. Why? Because it is well known that the only security we possess against the perpetuation of error, the only means for its final separation from truth, with which it always mixes itself more or less, is free discussion between unbiassed minds. But it has been decided otherwise in regard to religion. The BIBLE, that book in which all Christians " think they possess the means of eternal life," but about which experience has also forced Protestants, at least, to agree, that, like the simples employed in healing the body, it is exposed to great mismanagement;—the Bible, concerning which such furious contentions have taken place—the Bible alone must be applied according to *privileged systems*. Though the difficulty of establishing the sense of the Bible on subjects about which Christians have destroyed Christians without mercy, is attested by the blood of the victims, and the chances of error in the decisions which constitute the established orthodoxies may be calculated by the frenzy of the passions which attended those decisions—nevertheless, those systems must be perpetuated by the engagement of passions still more dangerous to truth and veracity than the pride and resentment which carried heretics to the stake. That the Roman Catholics, who have persuaded themselves that, by a perpetual miracle, no error was at any time permitted to form part of their Church's creed, should fence that creed with everything that can secure to it the awe and the attachment of both the clergy and the laity, is perfectly natural and intelligible. But that Protestants should continue to imitate the same conduct and practice, in respect to creeds, to interpretations of Scripture, in which all acknowledge that there may be errors, is one of the strangest inconsistencies which the history of civilized nations attests. In the mean time, and by the direct influence of this system, divisions, which time and reflection might heal, are rendered perpetual and incurable. Under these artificial securities, under these regular combinations of men, thus solemnly bound not to depart from a certain view of Scripture, no gradual approach to a brotherly conformity can be made. The general sense of Christians cannot be progressively ascertained by the transition of one body of men into another. If any one ventures to examine the points in question, he is obliged to weigh his doubts in secret, as if he were meditating a crime. To doubt any of the principal doctrines which are used as the colours of these compactly organized and disciplined bodies, is to meditate desertion; to deny their truth, is not a change of opinion—as in other disputed matters—it is joining the ranks of the most detested rebels. Under such circumstances, can there be a possibility of finally rendering the Scriptures what they should be—the bond of union among those who bear the name of Christians?

Alas! were it not for the baneful power of ORTHO-DOXY—of that pretended duty of agreeing with the doctrines which, at some earlier or later period, became the nucleus, the bond of a church party—we might long since have learned, by the united and freely compared experience of the Christian world, either what is the most natural sense of Scripture on the disputed doctrines, or (what is more probable) a general conviction might have been established, that the field of metaphysical speculation has been left free, in order that individuals may indulge their peculiar intellectual tendencies, provided they do not interfere with the opposite tendencies of others. But what we now possess is not the intellectual experience of the millions of Christians who, in the course of many centuries, have joined the various standards of belief: their assent has never been free and unbiassed—at least, we have strong reasons to suspect its freedom. The Christian world has been divided into proselyting parties, who, assisted by secular power, and frequently using or threatening violence, have recruited their ranks and prevented desertion by means totally unconnected with free and deliberate conviction. If, perchance, a certain number of individuals have really and fully coincided with the standard of faith adopted by their church, the early prepossessions in which they have been brought up, the spiritual terrors of heresy which have been deeply impressed on their minds (not to mention attractions and trammels of another kind), take away more than half the value of their testimony. We have, indeed, no reason to doubt the sincerity of individuals from general surmises. But though we highly respect the attainments and venerate the virtues of many who have been and are still solemnly bound to support the peculiar interpretations and doctrines of some particular church which definitely limits the sense of Scripture by articles, instead of qualifying the sense of those articles by the sense which the subscriber finds, or may find, in Scripture, we cannot consider the impression which the Scripture has left on their minds as an experimental instance of the natural sense or mental result of those books. The experiment, like many of those attested in the history of alchemy, has been made in a vessel not at all free from substances which ought not to have been there.

The free and unprejudiced mind dwells with delight on the image of the universal church or convocation of Christ, as it would naturally have grown "into the fulness of the body" of its glorious Founder, had not its growth been disturbed and distorted by the intolerant pride of ORTHODOXY. United by the acknowledgment of Jesus of Nazareth as our King, appointed by his Father to reign over his moral kingdom, till every tribe and nation shall confess that he is Lord, "to the glory of the Father;" agreed in the confession that, for every purpose of well-grounded hope connected with the future, and of all spiritual instruction required for the present life, he is "one with the Father;" professing to take his will and example as the rule and the pattern of their individual conduct; and confident in the promise he gave them of an eternal divine assistance to enlighten each upright conscience and strengthen each honest heart in the progressive attainment of moral conformity with his Master, so that he may be one with him, as Jesus and his Father are one;* adopting charity, *i.e.* mutual love and kindness, as the distinguishing sign and common bond of the Christian society; keeping Christ's declaration, that "his kingdom is not of this world," as a strong barrier against the mixture of temporal interests with the spiritual concerns of the Christian community;—under such circumstances, Christianity might have spread (as indeed it was intended to do, and as we have reason to hope that it will, in spite of obstacles) as a bond of fraternal love between the nations of the earth ; as a preservative against the fears of superstition, which still embitter the soul of man in every region under heaven, and poison his best natural tendencies ; as the support of one common hope of happiness in a future world; banishing from among the rational inhabitants of the earth the notion that ceremonies, sacrifices, and priestly interference, are necessary to please that great and good God, of whom the highest and truest thing that can be said, in human language, is, that he is a SPIRIT, and that he delights in those who worship him in *spirit* and in *truth;* cherishing the growth and full development of the faculties which distinguish us from the brutes ;—in a word, spreading and perfecting CIVILIZATION to the utmost limits of the inhabitable earth.

And what (let me earnestly and solemnly ask) has hitherto turned this view into a mocking dream—a dream which deludes by images which are the very reverse of the sad realities which surround us?—ORTHODOXY; the notion that the eternal happiness or misery of individuals is intimately connected with the acceptance or rejection of a most obscure system of

* John xvii. 11, 21, 22.

metaphysics; a system perplexing in the extreme to those who are best acquainted with its formerly technical, now obsolete language, and perfectly unintelligible to the rest of the Christian world; a system which, to say the least, *seems* to contradict the simplest and most primitive notions of the human mind concerning the unity, the justice, and the goodness of the Supreme Being; a system which, if it be contained in the Scripture, has been laid under so thick and impenetrable a veil, that thousands who have sought to discover it, with the most eager desire of finding it, whose happiness in this world would have been greatly increased by that discovery, and who, at all events, would have escaped much misery had they been able to attest it, even on grounds of probability sufficient to acquit themselves before their own conscience, have been compelled by truth to confess that they cannot see it. Yet Orthodoxy declares this very system identical with Christianity—with that gospel which was "preached to the poor" and "revealed unto babes:" such a system, we are told, is that faith which "*except every one keep whole and undefiled, without doubt he shall perish everlastingly.*"

By the influence of this Orthodoxy the world has been placed in a worse condition, for peace and mutual love, than it was before the gospel. Neighbouring tribes might, in ancient times, make their gods the pretext for indulging mutual jealousy. But the comprehensive religion of the Romans, though inexorable when a foreign system threatened to loosen the bonds of their political body (which, as experience proved, was the decided tendency of Christianity organized by Bishops into a political body, foreign to that under whose laws they lived), constantly bestowed protection on the religions of the conquered countries, and prevented, by this means, all attacks on each other. But observe the effects of Christianity identified with Orthodoxy. The earth reeks still from the torrents of blood which have been shed in the name of the gospel. And the error is plausible. It is true that the SPIRIT of the gospel itself opposes it; but it is of the very nature of Orthodoxy to direct the attention, not to the SPIRIT but to the letter; and the LETTER of the New Testament contains no express declaration against preventing heterodoxy by the infliction of punishment. That Jesus did not allow the two disciples to command fire from heaven against the Samaritans who would not receive him, is an example that might protect the unconverted heathen from Christian zealots; that he would not pray for twelve legions of angels to save him out of the hands of his enemies, only proves that "the cup he had to drink could not pass away from him." Yet, if the bond of his kingdom is Orthodoxy; if the eternal life of the subjects of that kingdom depends on the purity of their creed, and heresy murders their souls, there is nothing in the New Testament that opposes the use of effectual measures to counteract evils of that magnitude. The argument, that if death is the fit punishment for the murderer of the body, much more must it be deserved by him who murders the soul, has the force of demonstration for every orthodox people on the face of the earth. So it has acted among the orthodox of the most opposite parties; and so it would act at this moment, even among Protestants, if a stanch orthodox clergy were supported by a stanch orthodox people. The horrors of the Inquisition do not belong to Rome by any necessary connection between their Catholic tenets and their cruelty. If Roman Catholics have been prominent in the vast field of religious persecution, it is because they are in the same degree prominent in the belief of their exclusive Orthodoxy.

Nor could it be otherwise; for that mistaken Christianity which proclaims abstract creeds as the only sure pledges of eternal happiness in heaven, has the power of combining sincerity and tranquillity of conscience with the indulgence of the two most powerful passions —fear and angry pride. An ancient idolater who saw the object of his worship despised, would feel the insult as personal; but the mere act of neglecting his favourite altar for another, would not give him the slightest offence. He believed that certain practices and oblations were preferable to others in regard to his individual happiness, just as in Roman Catholic countries different persons choose the patronage of different saints, without a shadow of uneasiness arising from the various views and tastes of the devotees. But the Orthodox, of whatever denomination or creed he may be, cannot endure varieties of creed: and, indeed, it is not in the nature of things that he should. Every man's salvation, according to his view of the subject, depends upon unhesitating assent to certain propositions, of such a very abstract nature, so inconsistent with the most certain principles of human Reason, that even when they have been most assiduously forced upon the infant mind, they very frequently drop off, in spite of the most sincere efforts of the same mind in its maturity. *Fear* and *sympathy* are generally the guardians to whom the orthodox creed is entrusted. Its preservation depends, therefore, much more upon external impressions than upon conviction. Now, a man who should believe that his salvation was connected with his assent to a series of geometrical theorems which he had once demonstrated, would not be irritated by the disbelief of his neighbours. But the disbelief of others has an irresistible effect on the mind, when Reason is uneasy. The WILL, in the cases to which I allude, is invariably found to have encroached on the province of the UNDERSTANDING, and forced it to be silent. This powerful faculty, however, has submitted reluctantly; and will struggle for mastery at the approach of another intellect which enjoys its freedom, or at least does not drag chains so oppressive and galling. But since, according to the Orthodox, every doubt thus raised by sympathy, endangers his own salvation, how can his fears allow him to be tolerant? How shall he be able to endure the presence of the tempter? He must regard him with feelings similar to those which a direct emissary of Satan would raise.

I must, however, hasten to conclude this letter, leaving you to enlarge and unfold the hints already given, as well as those with which I shall close it.

You have only to cast a wide and comprehensive glance over the New Testament, to be convinced that the spiritual (*i.e.* mental) stamp of the gospel is LIBERTY. Christ is not only a SAVIOUR from SIN, but from SUPERSTITION—a word that properly embraces all religions which make ceremonies and a priesthood essential to spiritual safety. I do not exclude the Jewish religion. As far as it was established and sanctioned by God, it was intended for a people who, "owing to the hardness of their heart," required a moral system of education strongly mixed with the very faults to which they were nationally inclined—a most delicate process for the final attainment of good, which man has not knowledge enough to conduct, and which the infinite wisdom of God alone can conduct without the danger of fortifying and increasing the evil which, by a partial and temporary sanction, is to be finally extirpated. Christ came to deliver the world from that evil; "to deliver us from the yoke of the law," and from every yoke of a similar nature. But observe the earliest attempt to corrupt, and indeed, according to St. Paul, to nullify the gospel.* Hear the voice of the first inventors of DAMNATORY ORTHODOXY.† "And certain men who came down from Judea, taught the brethren (and said), Except ye be circum-

---

* "Behold, I Paul say unto you, that if ye be circumcised, Christ shall profit you nothing." Gal. v. 2.—The gospel, the glad tidings of deliverance, would, of course, be contradicted by the resumption of ceremonies as necessary to salvation.

† The declaration in Mark xvi. 16 (if the passage from ver. 9 to the end be genuine, which there is good reason to doubt), has been supposed to contain the principle of damnatory Orthodoxy; but, certainly, without foundation. The safety or salvation which the gospel promises is, as I have shewn before, attached to REPENTANCE (expressed by baptism or immersion, which signifies a moral *death* to past sinful courses, and a resurrection, or new *life*, to virtue), and the acceptance of the Christ as our moral guide. Condemnation, *i. e.* CENSURE (with the extent of its effects, I am not at present concerned), is declared to be incurred by those who, having had a sufficient attestation of the truth of the gospel, nevertheless reject it, and remain unrepentant. This is very different from the metaphysical Orthodoxy which dooms to eternal punishment such as will maintain their mental liberty against it. Matt. x. 14, 15, condemns the bigoted and disingenuous spirit which refuses so much as to *entertain*, to give *a hearing* to, persons who by fair and reasonable means wish to call our attention to views of religious subjects differing from our own.

cised after the manner of Moses, YE CANNOT BE SAVED."* These men understood the method of keeping up the religious dependence of the laity on the priesthood. FEAR is the very essence of superstition†, and superstition the chain by which the priest secures the people to himself. Hence, in all ages, the constant re-echoing of the words, *ye cannot be saved:* except ye be under the Pope, *ye cannot be saved:* except ye believe the Athanasian Creed, *ye cannot be saved*: except ye believe that the first sin of the first man utterly corrupted human nature, *ye cannot be saved:* except ye believe in predestination and imputed righteousness, *ye cannot be saved.*‡

How different was the language of the apostle Paul! How perfectly independent of such conditions was the salvation which he preached as "glad tidings." "Stand fast ... in the LIBERTY wherewith Christ hath made you free, and be not entangled again with the yoke of bondage."§ To demand either ceremonies, with the Jews; or mortifications, with the Ascetics; or belief in metaphysical theories, with the Theosophists‖ (three classes of men who "came in privily to spy out the Christians'

It is, in fact, a pointed declaration against the intolerant *Jewish Orthodoxy*. Let it be observed, besides, that the apostles had no complicated metaphysical creed to propose. Their message was, "The kingdom of heaven," *i. e.* the moral reign of God through the Messiah, "is at hand."

* Acts xv.

† Δεισιδαιμονία; or, as literally as it can be rendered, fear of the invisible powers.

‡ See note to page 34, at the end. The true sense of the original would not suit the purpose of intimidation in the degree required by corporate Orthodoxy; else the true translation of these and similar passages would only convey the idea of *not being right*, of *not being on the path of moral safety.*

§ Gal. v. 1. ‖ See Coloss. ii.

liberty,"* and to induce them to add to the gospel the views of their respective parties); to make salvation depend on anything external or internal, except that faith, that trust in the truths announced and sanctioned by Christ which shews itself in holiness of life, was, in Paul's eyes, to destroy the gospel. Even the Apostle James, who (whatever the blindness produced by a groundless theory of inspiration may obstinately assert) opposed Paul's too broad and too declamatory statements of justification by faith alone—even James was full of the leading notion that Christianity is "the law of liberty." But let us hear Paul again: "Where the spirit of the Lord is, there is liberty."† Orthodoxy has so blinded Christians, that many, I fear, will be ready to consider the application of this passage as a mere accommodation of the word *liberty* to my subject. I have, indeed, frequently remarked how seldom divines dwell upon this part of the Second Epistle to the Corinthians; how constantly they pass over that most significant sentence—"Who also hath made us able ministers of the New Testament; NOT OF THE LETTER, BUT OF THE SPIRIT; FOR THE LETTER KILLETH, BUT THE SPIRIT GIVETH LIFE." But is it not clear that, according to Paul, the New Testament or covenant, through Christ, has no LETTER? That it does not consist in words to be explained, in order to reach some abstruse sense as the substance of that covenant? The VAIL which remained "untaken away," in the reading of the Old Testament, "by the Jews," the "*vail* which is done away in Christ," the "vail" of the "letter that killeth," the cloud

---

* Gal. ii. 4, compared with Coloss. ii. † 2 Cor. iii. 17.

of WORDS which was afterwards made indispensable for salvation, remains, alas! upon the hearts of most Christians to this hour. It is, I am convinced, this *verbal faith*, this "letter that killeth," which ruins Christianity amongst us; which inspires most denominations of Christians with aversion, suspicion, and jealousy towards those who do not receive the *letter* of their creeds and articles; which makes the attempt to spread the gospel among the heathens an object of mockery in the eyes of many, who cannot but ridicule the idea of preaching abroad what is yet unsettled at home. Would heaven that Christians had their own "vail" of orthodox words taken away from their minds; that, limiting Orthodoxy to the acceptance of the Christ as the SPIRIT* ("*the Lord is that Spirit*," says St. Paul), *i.e.* the meaning, the end of all revelation, would not allow a new *letter*, consisting of abstract doctrines, to involve their minds in a "vail," which obstructs the view of the gospel, even more than the old letter which kept the Jews in bondage. Happy indeed would it be for the best interests of mankind, if

* That πνεῦμα, in opposition to γράμμα, can mean *spirit* only in the sense which contrasts with *letter*, seems too clear to require proof. Yet, if I am not much mistaken, πνεῦμα is, by some, understood in this passage in a mystical sense, as if conveying the notion that Christ is the *spirit*, the internal power which animates, strengthens, and enlightens the true believers; a sense, in my opinion, totally inconsistent with the context. According to Paul, in this place, the Christ is the *end*, τὸ τέλος, the final object of "that which is abolished," namely, the *letter* of the law; consequently he is the *thing meant*, the *spirit* of that *letter*. Upon this is grounded Paul's assertion, that whoever should turn towards Christ, *i.e.* the *spirit* or meaning of the *letter* of the Mosaic *law*, would have the "vail" which blinded the Jews taken away from his mind. Wherever that *meaning*, that *spirit of the Lord*, that true knowledge of the end of revelation, which centres in the Messiah, prevails, taking possession of the heart and mind, *there is liberty*.

all who glory in the name of Christians would turn away from the clouds of words that divide them into hostile parties; making the Christ, the Son of God, their point of union, and giving the right hand of fellowship to every one who, by obedience to the will of God, as we know it through our moral Lord and Master, shews that he *loves him in sincerity*. Then would the church of Christ be UNIVERSAL indeed: then would the spirit of the Lord be truly among us, and with it would appear spiritual LIBERTY attended by peace and charity: then might we hope to gain over many of those who, shocked by our present wranglings, turn away from him whom we misrepresent as the Founder of an unintelligible religion.

I conclude with an observation upon which, ever since it occurred to me, my mind has dwelt with unabated interest. I wish you to observe the connection of the notions SPIRIT and LIBERTY which appears in many parts of the New Testament, and especially in the passage on which I have made these remarks. But most particularly do I wish to draw your attention to that sentence (to me the most sublime that ever was expressed in human language) which the Christ addressed to the Samaritan woman. When that right-minded, though frail, creature shewed her eager desire for religious instruction, especially on the long-pending controversy between her own nation and the Jews, what was the answer? Does Jesus describe any new modification of the usual systems of religion? Does he speak of a new priesthood, of a new doctrine, of a new sacrifice? Far from it. "The hour cometh (he says in regard to the Messiah's kingdom) and now is, when the true worshippers shall worship the Father in *spirit* and in *truth*." TRUTH, in this passage, evidently means *reality*, in contradistinction to *emblems;* the worship of the heart, in opposition to the worship of ceremonies; the direct worship of the soul, not that which requires the interposition of a priesthood. But mark the *reason* given: GOD IS A SPIRIT. To the Eternal Mind (such is the reasoning implied), to that Eternal Being who is the Father of Spirits, the only acceptable worship must be that which is truly *spiritual.* Figures and ceremonies must cease; for they are shadows, and he loves realities. The only sacrifice he demands is that of the individual will to his Supreme Will. This is the *reasonable service* of faith peculiar to Christianity. But the mind, which is both the altar and the priest of this sublime and pure sacrifice, should not be degraded by a subjection to *words,* which are mere figures, more oppressive and enslaving than that of the Jews to the ceremonial law. The spirit of the Christ has set the spirit of the true worshipper completely free from such fetters. The Christian worshipper should worship in TRUTH; and nothing is true to the human mind but what carries conviction to the Reason: another man's truth is error to *him* who does not see it as true. To offer up such borrowed truth—a truth which the individual Reason rejects—is to lay a falsehood before God's throne as an offering. Such, in most cases, are the offerings of Orthodoxy.

LETTER III.

ON HERESY AND ORTHODOXY.

My dear Friend,

In my first Letter I defined Heresy, "an opposition to the various standards of Christian faith which men not only adopt for themselves, but also think binding on all others." This was the result of the reasoning which preceded the definition; and I consider it proved by that reasoning. I have, nevertheless, employed a great part of that first Letter, and the whole of the second, in confirming the accuracy of that analytical conclusion. But I am not yet satisfied that I have done enough. The difficulty of uprooting a prejudice which was almost undisturbed during, at least, fourteen centuries before the Reformation; a prejudice which the Reformers themselves, for the most part, confirmed; a prejudice which is instilled into the opening mind with the first rudiments of education; a prejudice, in fine, which in this country has become so disguised that it exists in full vigour side by side with the most active spirit of political freedom—the difficulty of uprooting such a prejudice is greater than anyone can conceive, who has not traced the minute ramifications by means of which it keeps its hold on men possessing the best qualities of mind and heart.

Do not lose sight, I again request you, of the leading principle which from the beginning I have laid before you. Heresy, in the sense which the different parties who call themselves Orthodox have given to that word, cannot be conceived unless it be proved that Christ established some perpetual authority—an authority to be kept in existence by an unquestionably legitimate succession—whose duty and privilege it is to declare what doctrines are true. If no such authority exists, if the Scriptures are addressed to the Reason and the Understanding, not of a privileged class, but of every individual who wishes to follow the Christ; if there is no divinely-appointed judge to decide between the various mental impressions, *i.e.* the various meanings which the Scriptures convey to different minds—Heresy is a word which expresses only the anger of one Christian against another. It is only in this light that a history of the Inquisition can be read without nourishing in ourselves an inquisitorial spirit. Excuse this repetition: the truth, in circumstances like those of my subject, glides off the mind as a paradox, unless it be repeatedly brought in contact with it, to be gradually, as it were, absorbed, and incorporated with the rest of our knowledge.

The same process should be adopted in regard to important passages of Scripture which, for many years, have been constantly presented to the mind in connection with *established doctrines*. Language being a collection of arbitrary signs and words, having no meaning but that which is given to them by the mental habits of those who use them, any word, and still more any sentence (for words in combination are particularly subject to a variety of shades of meaning), if habitually repeated in connection with certain notions, will appear to reject all other significations, as it were, by a *natural* power. The identical texts which opposite parties of Christians so decidedly assert to convey *naturally* and *obviously* notions which destroy each other, are (considering the sincerity with which those assertions are generally made) striking instances of the unlimited power of association over language. The controversialists stare, in unfeigned surprise, at what each conceives to be the glaring absurdity and perverseness of his opponent. The ill-subdued flames of equally genuine zeal make the blood boil in their veins when they observe that such *plain* words as body and blood, for instance, are not taken in their *obvious* sense; forgetting that in arbitrary signs, especially when they may be used *figuratively*, that sense alone can be obvious which use has rendered familiar.* For persons who belong to the same age and country, and who, by education and habits, have been placed in a sort of mental contact with the generations of their not very remote forefathers, the language of those ancestors may, in many cases, properly be said to have an *obvious* meaning. But in the very ancient languages, especially of the Eastern nations, there is hardly any expression which can have an obvious meaning for *us*. The habits of the Jews in Jesus's time, for instance, were so totally different from ours,

---

* At all events, that sense cannot be *obvious* which would not *stand before* or present itself readily, and without delay. If we heard a person, holding some bread in his hands, say, *This is my body*, the *literal* sense would by no means come foremost into our minds: it would not *stand before us*, or be obvious. This observation may be applied in very different ways, according to circumstances.

the mass of each individual's ideas was so dissimilar to that which will be found in a corresponding class of people among us, that the phrases which would convey a clear meaning to a child in those times, may now be grossly misunderstood by the ablest men. We have but one method of avoiding great mistakes in the perusal of such writings as those of the New Testament. The reader should make himself, as much as possible, a contemporary of the writers, by an intimate acquaintance with their language, their learning, their modes of thinking, and their habits. In this manner will he be able to understand the general import of those documents, especially in connection with *practical* subjects of morals; —*morals* I say, not limiting the word to *external* conduct, but extending it to the discipline of the *will* and affections. In regard to this, the notions of mankind are so coincident, that they may be conveyed even by the slightest hints.* But in respect to philosophical or speculative ideas, especially in relation to the invisible world, far from expecting that the sense of those writers should be *obvious*, a sober and unprejudiced mind will be prepared to meet with great obscurity. All that we have a right to expect is a *probable* sense, disclosed by the light which the clearer passages cast over the more obscure. But even this probability is greatly diminished by the habits of mind which are sedulously cherished in children, and which grow with them into manhood. The notions which some early

---

* It is owing to this that Homer's poems are easily understood, so far, at least, as to create a deep interest. The words of that patriarch of poetry have a living interpreter in every human heart. The same happens in regard to many portions of the Hebrew Scriptures.

writers conceived and published when knowledge was very scarce among Christians—the notions which, in subsequent times, a clergy who took for their mental guide a deceitful *verbal* philosophy, reduced into a logical system, with nothing but empty speculation for its ground—these notions digested into catechisms, whose expressions have been incorporated with every vernacular tongue, are now so attached, by mental association, to certain passages of Scripture, that it is very difficult to separate them, even when the understanding is thoroughly convinced that they could not be thus associated in the minds of the original teachers of Christianity.

That you may completely overcome such habits, allow me to recommend the re-perusal of such passages in the New Testament as speak of the SPIRIT in opposition to the LETTER, and of Christian LIBERTY in contrast with Jewish BONDAGE, examining them in the light of the principle which I have developed in the two preceding Letters. Examine, I beg you, whether, if the common notions of HERESY and ORTHODOXY were true, the law of Moses would be so decidedly inferior to the gospel as the Apostle Paul represents it; or whether, on the contrary, if, while our salvation depended on our right choice of *theological* opinions, and on the legitimate use of SACRAMENTS (as some practices are called, without the least ground or authority), we had been left in great uncertainty as to the truth of the opinions and the divine appointment of the ministers of the sacraments, we should not be in an infinitely lower condition than the Jews. Under the supposed necessity of embracing certain dogmas and receiving certain sacraments (the latter, of course at the hands of *legitimate* ministers), as conditions of salvation, our Christian LIBERTY ought rather to be called the Christian anarchy. It would be such liberty as that which sailors would enjoy upon a coast abounding in sunken rocks, when every lighthouse, and buoy, and signal, had been removed; or rather, when every family who lived in the neighbourhood had been allowed to set up lights, and to float buoys, according to their respective notions of the safe and the dangerous parts of those seas; and to distribute contradictory charts of soundings, which each family had tried with lines of some three feet in length.

The New Testament is, indeed, deprived of its very life on the usual supposition that Orthodoxy is identical with, or constitutes an essential part of, *saving faith*. That passage, in particular, which I paraphrased at the end of my second Letter, becomes a collection of empty sounds, if we admit that supposition. There is, indeed, but one sense in which it expresses a definite notion, in conformity with the meaning of the word Gospel (*i.e.* glad tidings), and presents a real contrast between the new and the old dispensation. Permit me to call again your attention to the third chapter of the second Epistle to the Corinthians, taking it up at the beginning till we come to that passage which I explained in my second Letter. But I wish to make one observation as an introduction to the exposition of the passage.

Had one of the principal offices of the apostles been, that of establishing such a VERBAL rule of faith as would have been indispensable for the existence of an association of men who were to depend on Orthodoxy for union in this world and for salvation in the next, the delivery of that RULE would certainly have been their most solemn and public act. If, to settle the question concerning the deference which Gentile proselytes owed to the law of Moses (so long as the Mosaic polity existed), the apostles issued a formal decree, preceded by a mature and public deliberation, how can it be imagined that they would have omitted to publish some such creed as that which was afterwards attributed to them, if they had been persuaded *by inspiration* that an acceptance of such articles was necessary to the attainment of eternal happiness? Both the appearance of the pretended Creed of the Apostles, about the time when the notion of articular Orthodoxy as identical with saving faith began to be general, and the non-existence of a real Apostles' Creed before that period, combine to prove irrefragably the un-apostolic character of that notion.

But in the passage to which I again call your attention, we have a more direct and positive proof that Paul's views were quite opposite to the notion in question. His apostolic authority having been disputed at Corinth, and again recognized in consequence of the effect produced by the first of his Epistles addressed to that Christian community, and of the exertions of his faithful friend Titus; this second Letter contains, as it might be expected, numerous observations on the legitimacy of his apostleship. Most, however, of these observations are rather attributable to bursts of feeling, which the writer is desirous to check, than to a deliberate intention of recommending himself to the Corinthians. At that point of the Letter which, according to our arbitrary divisions of the text, we call the beginning of the third chapter, the writer suspects that he is addressing his reconciled Corinthian converts in the tone of self-commendation. He accordingly checks himself, though not without hinting at the mean arts of his rivals, who used, it seems, to procure commendatory letters to the various Christian assemblages, among whose members they were anxious to gain popularity. Paul, remembering this unworthy method of canvassing for the favour of those whom, with so much labour, he had "begotten to Christ," expresses a well-grounded confidence that he himself was above the necessity of procuring recommendations to his own spiritual children. "Others (I express his meaning) may want letters introducing them to your favour; but in yourselves I have a LETTER which much exceeds all other such writings in value. The world may read in YOU one of my clearest titles to the apostleship of which some interested and envious men would deprive me. You, Corinthians, appear before the world as an epistle of Christ, in my favour. You are a *letter*, written, not with ink, but with the spirit of the living God; not in tables of stone, like those which attested the mission of Moses, but in the fleshly tables of the heart, whereupon we, the apostles of Christ, are commissioned to engrave the law of the Spirit."

As soon, however, as the idea of a contrast between the old and the new dispensation arises in the apostle's mind, he seizes it with his usual eagerness, and gives his readers a lesson on which Christians cannot dwell too long or too intensely. "God (I continue to give the meaning of Paul's words) has made us ministers of the new covenant, under a character entirely opposite to that of the mission of Moses. The law which Moses was sent to proclaim and establish was LITERAL: that which we are publishing to the world has no LETTER: it is a law of PRINCIPLE; and herein consists the superiority of the gospel above the law. A *literal* law is a burden which deadens the human mind; a *spiritual* law, on the contrary, adds activity and power, especially under the influence of that spirit of life which we have received, and of which we, the original preachers of the gospel, have been appointed ministers. This is our title to the authority we claim of bearing witness to Christ, as his peculiar messengers, and to the honour due to that office. For if Moses received honour from God, though he was the minister of a *literal* law, from which the people subject to it could expect nothing but a constant sense of transgression, and the blame (the condemnation) of the law which they broke, how much more must our ministry be entitled to glory and honour, whose office is to proclaim a covenant which does not depend on VERBAL or LITERAL statutes, but which, announcing the spirit of the Lord Jesus, which is a spirit of LIBERTY, invites mankind to cast off the yoke of statutes and ordinances of all kinds relating to religion, and thus to be free from all sin and the fear of sin!—a freedom which the most religious observers of the law of Moses, even when totally devoted to the fulfilment of the conditions of the Mosaic covenant, could not attain."

If this be the reasoning contained in the passage before us (as I trust you will find it upon due consideration, especially in connection with the portion of the same chapter which I explained in my second Letter), what can be more plain and direct than the inference, that the apostle Paul considered the gospel as being subject to no LITERAL conditions, to demand no obedience to LITERAL PRECEPTS?—Now, I ask, is this

LIBERTY consistent with the pretended law of Orthodoxy? Can any obedience be more burdened with verbal precepts and limitations than the dogmatic faith on which the various parties, called churches, will have salvation to depend? Precepts laid upon the mental faculties—LITERAL, VERBAL directions to the understanding, compelling Reason to admit certain propositions as true, in spite of the total indefiniteness of the impressions conveyed by the words, in opposition to previously established principles, and under the absolute necessity of taking the most inadequate material figures for the objects which they are said to represent—such precepts are infinitely more burdensome than the whole Levitical law. The laws of sacrifice, of external purity, and of difference of meats, were definite and intelligible. The man who submitted to them was morally a slave; but he might know how far he had succeeded in the fulfilment of his ceremonial task. But if the most important part of the gospel (as it is represented) consisted of intellectual PRECEPTS,—propositions directing Christians, upon pain of damnation, "how they are to think" (as the Athanasian Creed tells us*) upon things beyond all the power of thought, we should be "of all men most miserable." We might well envy the condition of the Jew, who, though loaded with precepts, could know with certainty whether he obeyed or failed. But how can we, when we embrace one particular Orthodoxy, be sure that we have not chosen a belief the very opposite of that which the metaphysical rule of right thinking, on what is beyond the pale of reason,

* Whosoever will be saved, must thus think of the Trinity.—*Athan. Creed.*

intended? The Jew (to mention one out of a multitude of instances) well knew the composition of the *Water of Separation;* but what prophet can quiet men's scruples as to the ingredients of a creed that shall contain neither more nor less than the true metaphysical deductions which may be drawn from the *letter* of the Old and the New Testament? The letter that killeth is declared by Paul not to belong to his ministry: could he, then, have been the minister of a dogmatic faith—of that double-edged sword which for so many centuries is supposed to have been killing souls—aye, and bodies too—to right and left? Could he preach the accursing, the anathematizing gospel of Councils, Popes, and Synods, Catholic and Protestant, ancient and modern? Can any mortal calculate the millions of millions of souls which must at this moment be irrevocably sunk in everlasting perdition, if the LETTER of the various Orthodoxies has been allowed to kill according to the wishes of their respective supporters?—if heresy be "a sin unto death"?

But let us suppose, for a moment (though I fear to weaken the impression of this argument), that St. Paul and his fellow-labourers, the other apostles, immediate disciples of Christ, had preached a dogmatic faith, the genuineness of which was to be proved by its conformity with some LETTER, *i.e.* some declaration in writing. Where did that declaration exist? When did the apostles deliver it to the Christian world as the rule of its faith throughout all future ages? The law of Moses, because it depended upon the letter of the law, was solemnly delivered to the people of Israel, to be preserved and transmitted by means of authenticated documents; but when was anything of this kind performed by the apostles, much less by Christ himself?

Nothing is more difficult, when we treat of events which took place at a very distant period, than to divest ourselves of our modern notions, and never to lose sight of the then existing circumstances. We are so accustomed to see the Old and New Testament bound together, and to regard that collection as an individual book, written for the express purpose of establishing Christianity, that I fear many will be misled, in the present question, by the notion that St. Paul must have referred his converts to their BIBLE. That he referred the *Jews* to the Old Testament for predictions of the Messiah, *i e.* for the conformity of the character described in those books with the character of Jesus of Nazareth, is certain; but we do not find that he recommended the same search to the Gentiles. Such a search, considering the difficulty and expense of obtaining manuscripts in those days, must have been impracticable to by far the greater part of the Gentile converts, even when we take in such as had learned to read, and could understand the translation of the Septuagint. If the Christian society at Corinth, a wealthy, refined, and *learned* city, contained not many wise men after the flesh, not many mighty, not many noble,* how few, capable of instruction by reading, must have been found among the semi-barbarian countries of Asia Minor, Phrygia, Cappadocia, Galatia, Pontus—in a word, all the country except a few Greek cities!

Now, in regard to the New Testament, we must not

* 1 Cor. i. 26.

forget that the writings to which we give that name did not exist, *as a collection*, for a considerable time after the publication of Christianity: in fact, the CAUSE of their being made up into a collection was the great increase of converts to the religion of Jesus. We must also remember, that when our present New Testament was *collected*, there was not one of the apostles alive who could authoritatively deliver it as the *verbal* rule of faith to the Christian world. But *suppose* the collection known to the apostle John. He lived a long time at Ephesus, where the wildest notions on religion were afloat. He met with a most violent opposition, and was excommunicated by Diotrephes, who probably justified his conduct to the church by accusing John of some essential error.* His first two Epistles are full of complaints against that class of Gnostics who denied the reality of Christ's person. What could be more natural, in such circumstances, than to appeal to, and fully explain, the nature of the RULE which, from that time till the end of things, was to settle controversies of faith in the universal church? But it is remarkable that not only does not John refer to any such rule, but, even when he was *not received* by a church, he does not assert his right to be acknowledged as a supreme judge of disputed questions. Nay, in a part of his first Epistle where he expressly cautions his disciples against men whom he calls ANTICHRISTS, men who had gone out from among St. John's society of Christians, and who, in the orthodox sense of the word, might properly be called HERETICS, the apostle

---

* "I wrote unto the church; but Diotrephes, who loveth to have the pre-eminence among them, *receiveth us not*." 3 John v. 9. This letter of John is one of the apostolic writings which has been lost.

appeals—to what? To his own inspiration? To some fixed standard of faith? No such thing. He refers to the JUDGMENT OF EACH INDIVIDUAL CHRISTIAN. "Ye have an unction (he says) from the Holy One, and ye know all things. I have not written unto you because ye know not the truth, but because ye know it, and that no lie is of the truth..... Let that therefore abide in you which ye have HEARD (no written documents mentioned) from the beginning.... These (things) have I written unto you concerning them that seduce you (no worse heretics in the modern sense could be described); but the anointing which ye have received of him abideth in you: and *ye need not that any man teach you.*"* Can any one conceive that this address was made under the persuasion that Jesus had intended to secure his gospel, and the benefits arising from it, by a RULE of logical and metaphysical Orthodoxy? I leave the answer to the common sense and conscience of every unperverted mind.

I have now stated some of the plainest *facts* which are attested in the New Testament; and they fully oppose the notion, that the collection to which we give that name was prepared *with a view* to the controversies which have divided the church from the first days of Christianity to this moment. This being true in regard to the New Testament, who can think that the Hebrew Scriptures were appointed for that purpose?

I trust I need not remind you that the Roman Catholic evasion—the supposition of a perpetual, living, and infallible judge of the Scriptures—has been totally demolished by the Protestant writers. The very existence

* 1 John ii.

of such a flimsy theory is a superabundant proof of the great truth for which I have been contending; for since the necessity of such a living judge arises from the notion that Christian faith necessarily implies ORTHODOXY, the evident non-existence of such a judge proves the falsity of the notion, upon the admittance of which the judge becomes absolutely necessary. God, we certainly know, would not make anything necessary for salvation, unless he had put that thing within the reach of every sincere inquirer after it. SAVING FAITH is, therefore, not ORTHODOXY. I know no proposition in divinity of which I feel more assured.

I request you now to fix an undivided attention on the inevitable consequence of the truth which I have established. If no living authority has been divinely established to explain the Scriptures on disputed points, is it not clear that those writings have been addressed equally to all men, in order that every one may endeavour to make out their sense by comparing different passages, and trying the explanations which he hears from others by the general SPIRIT of those Scriptures? In other words, is it not evident that God has left the sense of the Scriptures, as far as that sense is of practical importance, free to every sincere Christian, and entirely to the judgment of his REASON? Can any other judge be proved to exist? The answer is placed beyond all doubt. The independence of human reason from all responsibility, except that which man feels in his inmost soul to the Eternal Fountain of that reason, is demonstrated.

It is said, that God has promised his Spirit to those who ask for it. This is perfectly true. It is a truth well known to all honest men who have examined the only *spiritual* world accessible to man—the world within us. Hear the memorable words of Seneca, words not unworthy to stand side by side with the best passages of St. Paul: *Sacer intra nos spiritus sedet, malorum bonorumque nostrorum observator et custos; hic, prout a nobis tractatus est, ita nos ipse tractat.** It is this universal Law, this fact of God's moral world, which the writers of the New Testament exhibit more or less under a clothing of that supernaturalism in which the Jews of that age and country saw all things. But the gift of the SPIRIT, that *unction* of which St. John speaks† · (probably in allusion to the anointment of the Hebrew priests, the interpreters of the old Law), was not intended as a check, but as a GUIDE‡ to the rational mind of man. The Divine Spirit of TRUTH has been promised to sincere Christians (I firmly believe it is promised to all honest men) to guide them in all that concerns their moral safety. The two SPIRITS—the Spirit (*i. e.* the mind, so we may call it without irreverence) of God, and the spirit of man, though infinitely apart from each other in their nature, are clearly represented by Paul as analogous (I might say *akin*) to each other.§ Nor could it be

* *Ad Lucil.* "A holy spirit has his seat within us, watching what in us is evil, and guarding what is good. He treats us as we have treated him."

† In the passage of his 1st Epistle, quoted before.

‡ "He will *guide* you into all the truth," namely, of the simple gospel.

§ "Likewise the Spirit also helpeth our infirmities: for we know not what we should pray for as we ought; but the Spirit itself maketh intercession for us (with sighs not expressed in words);" *i. e.* the divine impulse after holiness which is in us, makes us sigh for what we cannot express; but God, who gives us that Spirit, knows what it is we wish for.

otherwise, since the one is the fountain-head of reason, the other a derived stream. Let us not, however, be misled by taking reason in the sense of some of its lesser powers or manifestations. By REASON in its highest sense—in that sense which Paul seems to convey when he speaks of that *spirit of man* which the *Spirit of God* assists, and with which the Divine intelligence sympathizes—we should understand that part of human nature, that *multiform* faculty, which constitutes man a RATIONAL being.* It is to this spirit of man—*i.e.* to his RATIONALITY, as opposed to everything which he has in common with brutes (a collective notion which St. Paul calls the FLESH)—that the Spirit of Christ, or that Spirit of God which is eminently in the Christ, is promised as a guide whenever the human will shall desire its influence. Yet the character in which this guide acts must unquestionably be that of REASON. Whatever theories may be conceived in regard to the manner of *inspiration*—visions, voices, internal impulses—the *reason* of the individual must be convinced of its reality, else it could not be distinguished from insanity. Everything *not reasonable,* either in itself or by virtue of the *ground* upon which we accept it, is *absurd*. REVELATION can have no authority for a rational being till REASON has recognized it as such.

To REASON, therefore, every Christian must address himself, in order to *prove all things, and hold fast that which is good*. Paul, who gave to his converts this highly *rational* direction, must have been perfectly aware of

---

* "The consideration I shall have of it (Reason) here ... is as it stands for a faculty in man—that faculty whereby man is supposed to be distinguished from beasts, and wherein it is evident that he surpasses them." *Locke on the Human Understanding,* b. 4, c. xvii.

the inalienable rights which the Supreme Source of the intellectual faculties has conferred upon human reason. He never speaks in the tone of an oracle to which reason must bow without examining its claims. "I speak as to wise men; judge ye what I say."* From the bold assumption of oracular infallibility, and the attempt to strike awe into the minds of those they address, the writings of Christ's apostles are perfectly free. That sort of language is characteristic of the pretenders to inspiration. Such is the tone constantly assumed by Mahomet. "There is no doubt in this book," is the first declaratory sentence in the Koran.†

There are no attempts in the New Testament to paralyze the reason of man. Throughout that collection of writings, the Spirit of God, as it manifests itself in the Christ and his apostles, appears with the tone and character of a friend, a helper which feels for, and identifies itself with, the spirit of man. Every one is earnestly invited, not indeed to quench his own spirit, but to exert its powers so as not to *quench* in himself the mild flame of the Spirit of God.

God dwells in every man by that direct ray of divine light called *reason* (I speak of the highest part of reason), as in his temple. This indwelling of the Deity, this presence of the Supreme Reason, may be truly asserted of all mankind. The *Logos*, the Divine Reason (of which, in regard to religion, Jesus is the human representative), is the "true light, which lighteth every man that cometh into the world."‡ But it is the peculiar power of Christianity—the religion of the Christ, which is the same as the *Logos*, which again is the same as the Divine Wisdom

---

* 1 Cor. x. 15.   † Sale's Koran, c. ii.   ‡ John i. 9.

HERESY AND ORTHODOXY. 77

or Intelligence—not only to remove the impurities which obscure that ray of divine light, but also to enlarge the capacity of the human mind, so as to make it more fit, by that moral purity which in Scripture language is called sanctification, to be the dwelling of that *rational* and *holy* presence which in figurative language is called the Holy Spirit, the Spirit of God, God himself.*

The invitations of the gospel are all addressed to the intelligent, moral part of man—to his *practical reason.* " *Consider* what I say (is St. Paul's language to Timothy), and the Lord give thee *understanding* in all things."† The word here used by the apostle, σύνεσις *(synesis)*, expresses the highest, the essential faculty of the *spirit* of man. By that faculty must the free, the accountable agent, Man, be *ultimately* guided, whatever assistance, *i.e.* whatever increase of *rationality*, he may receive from the Fountain of reason; otherwise he would not be a free agent.‡

May the time soon arrive when the notion of a natural opposition between REASON and REVELATION shall be exploded! The "carnal mind, which is enmity against God," is not REASON, but its very opposite. It is the animal part of man. When this animal part, with its

---

* "Know ye not that ye are the temple of God, and that the Spirit of God dwelleth in you?"—1 Cor. iii. 16, 17. This is a sublime truth, in which *true* philosophy coincides with the spirit of the New Testament. That St. Paul understood by God, or his Spirit, the *rational* part of man, that part of us which partakes of the Divine nature, seems to me clear from the conclusion which the writer draws against encouraging the mere animal propensities. "If any man (he concludes) *defile* the temple of God, him shall God destroy." No argument is so powerful against animal degradation as that which arises from our *rationality.*

‡ 2 Tim. ii. 7. ‡ See note at the end.

blind appetites, has, by a determination of the will, been submitted to the law of the SPIRIT (which is the law of pure, divine REASON, the law of the Logos or Christ)—when it has been placed under the law of Christian motives, of Christian filial love to God, as we know him through the Christ—that moment our SPIRIT, our superior or mental portion, which is properly *ourselves*, begins the process of identification with the Spirit of God, that assisting power which "helps our infirmities: from that moment we are in the way of *safety*, we are SAVING OURSELVES, σωζόμενοι (*soozomenoi*). If, nevertheless, our reason, though sincerely placed by our will under the guidance of the Spirit of God, still rejects tenets which other Christians declare to be necessary to salvation—if our SPIRIT cannot be "fully persuaded" that such doctrines are contained in the Scriptures—we need not be alarmed at the clamour of the Orthodox, for unquestionably they have not been appointed to be our judges.

I will conclude with one of the many passages in St. Paul's Epistles which would place the intellectual or spiritual liberty of Christians beyond doubt, were it not for the thick mist which the established theological prejudices have cast over the Scriptures. The words which I am about to quote relate to a question considered as of vital importance in St. Paul's time. The observance or non-observance of the Law in connection with the hopes of salvation given by the gospel, was then an essential point in controversy. I ardently pray that Christians of all denominations may imbibe the spirit of St. Paul's advices relating to that question, and apply it to our present divisions. "Him that is weak in the faith receive, but not to doubtful disputations... Who art thou that judgest another man's servant?.... But why dost thou judge thy brother? or why dost thou set at nought thy brother? for we shall all stand before the judgment-seat of Christ... so then every one of us shall give an account of himself to God. *Let us not therefore judge one another any more; but judge this rather, that no man put a stumbling-block, or an occasion to fall, in his brother's way."** How many, alas! are daily made to fall away from the Christ by the stumbling-block of ORTHODOXY!

* Rom. xiv.

LETTER IV.

ON HERESY AND ORTHODOXY.

My dear Friend,

The word Heresy, among Christians, is derived from the New Testament.* If we consult the nine passages in which αἵρεσις (*hairesis*) is used by the sacred writers, and the only one in which a heretic† is mentioned, we shall find the word in question representing various notions, all of which have a common basis—namely, the idea of dissension occasioned by individual choice. All

---

* The word αἵρεσις appears not unfrequently in the classical Greek writers, meaning a philosophical school or sect. Plutarch, whose style, owing to the period when he wrote (he died in an advanced old age about A.D. 140), may be used as a commentary on the style of the writers of the New Testament, uses the word in question in a sense well worthy of attention. At the beginning of the same Life to which I have made reference in a note, he says of both Timoleon and Æmilius Paulus, that they were men—οὐ μόνον ΤΑΙΣ ΑΙ'ΡΕ΄ΣΕΣΙΝ, ἀλλὰ καὶ ταῖς τύχαις ἀγαθαῖς ὁμοίως κεχρημένων ἐπὶ τὰ πράγματα. The Langhornes give *virtues* for "αἱρέσειν," and translate, rather loosely, "men famous not only for their virtues but for their success." The true meaning is, that they were men who brought to the management of affairs not only excellent PRINCIPLES, but also great good luck. Here "αἱρέσεσιν" means the result of choice and deliberation.

† Acts v. 17, xv. 5, xxiv. 5, 14, xxvi. 5, xxviii. 22; 1 Cor. xi. 19; Gal. v. 20; 2 Peter ii. 1. The word αἱρετικός (*haireticos*) is found only in Tit. iii. 10.

such unions as we call, in some cases sects, in other parties, were or might be named αἱρέσεις (*haireseis*). That name did not necessarily imply reproach, nor the maintenance of erroneous doctrines as a bond of the union. The first connection of the word heresy with reproach, in the language of the Apostle Paul, arises from the notion of practical discord and dissension. Paul, indeed, uses the words divisions and heresies as equivalent. "I hear (he says to the Corinthians, 1 Cor. xi. 18 and 19) that there are divisions among you; and I partly believe it; for there must be also heresies among you."* This sense of the word had not become quite obsolete even at so late a period as the fifth century. Chrysostom, in the beginning of that century, and Theodoret, in the middle of it, explained the passage of St. Paul, just quoted, as one in which *dissensions*, not dogmatic errors, were deprecated by the apostle.†

But the abuse which finally reduced the word heresy to the signification of damnable error, began at a very early period. The age in which Christianity appeared was one of metaphysical speculation. Those who, like the learned, pious, and philosophical *Neander*, have attentively studied whatever documents, both of oriental and occidental literature, are preserved relative to that

---

* The addition also of καί may appear, at first sight, to establish an important distinction between divisions and heresies, but the context shews the contrary. The only distinction which it admits is, perhaps, that of accidental dissensions (σχίσματα, *schismata*), and permanent or regularly formed parties (αἱρέσεις).

† Lardner quotes the following words from Suicer, under the word Αἵρεσις: Diximus vocem αἱρέσεως hac tertiâ significatione sumi, 1 Cor. xi. 19. Hic tamen dissimulandum non est, veteres non intelligere doctrinam orthodoxiæ contrariam, sed contentiones, &c.—*Lardner*, Vol. IV. p. 506, edition in 5 vols.

period, have discovered the clearest proofs of an universal excitement, a vehement longing for disclosures concerning the moral nature of man, his hopes and his fears (inasmuch as these transcend the narrow limits of this life), which, more or less, pervaded all classes of men in all civilized countries. This mental restlessness was not confined to the East. Rome itself exhibited the same ferment of mind in the rage for foreign mysteries and initiations, which invited to that capital crowds of priests from the most distant parts of the empire. The senate, at an earlier period, and the emperors, at that of which I am speaking, were often alarmed by this spirit: and no deep reading in the works of the first, second, and third centuries is required to be acquainted with the fact, that the Mathematici, *i.e.* professors of divination by means of numbers, charms, and astrology, obtained a most powerful influence at Rome, for which they not unfrequently paid dearly in banishment and other punishments.

The ardent imaginations of the Eastern people were, however, the most appropriate receptacle for every speculative extravagance. From a remote period, various systems of theological doctrines had existed among the orientals, which, under different shapes and modifications, may still be recognized as descended from a common origin, and may be traced back to the regions of the Indus and Ganges. Even the Jews, who, from the nature of their religious and political constitution, might have been supposed to be out of the reach of everything which did not originate in Moses, could not escape the general infection. But the captivity which the mass of the nation underwent in Assyria, brought the Jews into a close contact with the learned Chaldeans, who at Babylon cultivated a branch of one of the principal stems of Indian philosophy. From Babylon, therefore, was derived that doctrine, afterwards called the Cabbala, on the knowledge of which some Rabbis of our Saviour's time built their highest claims to celebrity. It is true that there were essential differences between what we may call the mystic systems of the Jews and those of other Eastern nations. Yet the Eastern Gnosis, as well as the traditional science of the Rabbis, had this important character in common—that the adepts in both boasted of their being in possession of secret and mysterious traditions, which, carrying conviction in themselves, scorned argumentative proof; and by means of which, not only were the secrets of creation and the source of physical and moral evil disclosed, but men were put in possession of several ultra-mundane facts, and of fixed laws connected with those facts, by means of which the initiated were enabled to perform the greatest wonders within the limits of this lowest of all the departments of creation, which has been allotted to mankind.

In such a state of things, it was most natural that the appearance of so very extraordinary a person as Jesus of Nazareth, the accounts of whose life abound in miracles, whose birth was narrated with circumstances which made it appear a *physical* effect of causes beyond the limits of this material world; who was reported to speak of himself as having come down from a sphere of existence raised far above this of ours, where sin, and pain, and death, bear rule;—on the appearance of such a teacher, followed by the preaching and the reported miracles of his immediate disciples, it was most natural that the attention of all the speculatists of the age should be turned to Christianity, and that, finding it infinitely better grounded than their own baseless systems, they should endeavour to use it as a foundation for those systems. You must have observed how the great physical discoveries of our times have been seized upon by various classes of theorists, in the common hope that every one should find in oxygen, galvanism, magnetism, or whatever new agent had come to view, the very corner-stone of his respective theory. At a time when the human mind worked entirely upon itself, and philosophers were universally agreed in giving external or objective existence to whatever their minds conceived as necessary—in other words, which will probably be more familiar to you—at a time when philosophy consisted in an unbounded system of Realism, which to every idea of the mind gave an independent existence in the universe, nothing could be more acceptable than a tangible point, a standing-place, upon which those mighty fabrics of the imagination, those theosophical systems, which were vended about as mysteries of the highest interest and value to man, might repose. Thus it happened in regard to the Gospel. Christianity had been published only a very few years, when all the mystic and speculative sects in Syria commenced a series of efforts to incorporate the Gospel with their own tenets, and to graft their peculiar notions on the young and vigorous stock whose branches they could not but perceive were about to spread far and wide. Although the writers in the New Testament do not mention the name of any philosophical sect, except the Pharisees and Sadducees, it is clear to those acquainted with the doctrines of Eastern philosophy, that the notions from which Paul especially apprehended a danger to the simplicity of the Gospel, belonged to those mystic systems which, in some instances combined with Judaism, in others directly opposing it, were widely diffused, soon after, under the name of Gnosis.

But no warnings were sufficient to prevent a rapid growth of the evil which that apostle feared and opposed. Men whose resources for wealth and distinction lay in the admiration of the multitude, saw a most favourable opportunity of rising in the world by availing themselves of the ardour with which the primitive converts had embraced the Gospel. Vain babblers, pretending to a deep and extensive knowledge of the invisible world, flocked to the infant Christian communities; and such was their power over the ignorant and simple minds which made up the great majority of those societies, that the founders of them found it difficult to maintain their own authority against them. Paul's distressing difficulties at Corinth are too vividly and feelingly described in his two Epistles to the church of that great city, to require assistance from another pen. But no tolerably well-instructed reader of the New Testament can doubt that Paul's rivals belonged to the class of Judeo-philosophical speculatists. Paul's express determination to lay down all claim to that kind of knowledge which our version denominates wisdom ($\sigma o \phi \iota a$, *sophia*), and to confine his teaching to the doctrine of "Jesus Christ, and him crucified," clearly points out by contrast what kind of preaching had seduced the minds of his converts. It is true that the apostle mentions the names of James, Cephas, and Apollos, men who seem to have been guiltless of the spirit of party which made use of their names to oppose the authority of Paul. That the persons thus named were not really leaders of those divisions, is proved by the appearance of Paul's own name as the watchword of a party. Even the name of Christ was, we find, used for a similar purpose. The fact seems to have been, that when various intruders undertook to reduce the Gospel to a philosophical system, each of them pretended to build his own speculations on the peculiar views—sometimes real, sometimes supposed —of the persons whose names they adopted as a party distinction.

Besides the many remarkable passages of the two Epistles to the Corinthians, in which Paul's renunciation of all scientific teaching pointedly marks, in his rivals, a dangerous affectation of deep philosophy, there is a circumstance in the notices preserved concerning Apollos which is strongly confirmatory of my view, that the attempts of various teachers to theorize on Christianity was the chief source of Paul's anxiety. It is on record[*] that Apollos was a native of Alexandria, the great seat of speculative philosophy at that period. This fact alone would be a fair ground for conjecturing that he belonged to the numerous class of Alexandrian Jews who, like Philo, united the study of the Old Testament with the idealistic and mystic system which was taught in the schools of that great city. But this conjecture will grow almost into certainty when the word which in the English version is translated *eloquent*, shall be expressed by

[*] Acts xviii. 24.

learned, which gives the true sense of λόγιος (*logios*) in that passage.*

In the public disputations with the Jews, Apollos must have found it necessary to employ all the subtleties of the Alexandrian school in defence of Christianity. He may at a subsequent period have been checked by Paul in the use of weapons which, though of service in dialectic contests, would be eventually injurious to the simplicity of the Christian system. But vain and light-minded Christians would naturally be allured by the public triumph of the Alexandrian, to imitate, and (as second-rate minds will always do) to exaggerate Apollos's manner and method. As we have the most powerful reasons to believe that Apollos himself was not actually at the head of an anti-Paulistic party, but remained in close friendship with the apostle, we may safely conclude that his name was adopted for the purpose of expressing the nature of the system which his imitators professed to follow. In a similar manner we must conceive that the names of James (who, as the local president of the congregation of Jerusalem, could not reside at Corinth) and of Cephas (who, as the apostle of the circumcision, is not likely to have ever

* Neander, from whose instructive and interesting history of the apostolic age—*Pflanzung und Leitung der Christlichen Kirche durch die Apostel*—I borrow this remark, observes that the peculiar service rendered by Apollos to the Christians was that of *confuting* the Jews in public disputations—εὐτόνως γὰρ τοῖς ’Ιουδαίοις διακατηλέγχετο—an ability which depends much rather on dialectics and metaphysics than on eloquence. Neander confirms the above-given signification of λόγιος by two passages, one of Josephus, de Bello Jud. vi. c. v. § 3, and another of Philo, de Vita Mosis, i. § 5. Josephus uses the word λόγιοι in opposition to ἰδιῶται. Three words of Philo are enough to shew that he agrees in the same signification : Αἰγυπτίων οἱ λόγιοι.

been in Greece) were taken by other portions of the Corinthian church, under the guidance of teachers who respectively pretended to follow the views which they described as peculiar to each of those distinguished apostles.

When once the notion that an essential part of Christianity consists in a system of speculative doctrines began to take root, it must have made a very rapid progress. A Christian teacher, full of the true spirit and power which Jesus promised for the purpose of announcing the simple and sublime truth of salvation through him, might easily employ a long life in announcing these "good tidings" to a world morally sinking under the double pressure of vice and superstition. But the case of a *nominal* Christian preacher is quite different. In both ancient and modern times, the *sounding brass* and *tinkling cymbals* among the Christian teachers have deeply felt the necessity of abstract theories to raise and maintain their personal importance. The heathen priesthoods were indispensable to heathen nations, on the ground that priests alone possessed the mysterious knowledge of the numerous and intricate performances by which the gods were rendered propitious. But Christ had appointed no *priesthood*. Nevertheless, there soon arose a notion that the presidents and directors of Christian congregations must be equivalent to the *priests* of other religions. But here, again, the absence of complicated ceremonies left this class of men without an office so peculiar to them as to make them indispensable to the unofficial part of the community. How, then, could the ambitious and worldly-minded rest satisfied in such a position? We know that they did not. The supposed necessity of both mysterious doctrines and mysterious ceremonies was soon set afloat by Christian teachers of that class of which Paul, James, and John, complain in their writings. The materials for such speculations were already present in great abundance. The Old Testament, on the one hand, had become for a very great part of the Jewish nation, and especially for the Alexandrian Jews, a collection of allegories; numerous theories about a long series of incorporeal emanations from God, were, on the other hand, the favourite subject of the then prevalent philosophy. In these circumstances it was, that speculations about the nature of the Christ had their origin. I shall here introduce to your notice only one instance of these speculative corruptions, as a specimen of a numerous class of errors which infested Christianity during the first three centuries.

One of the earliest heresies (I shall now use that word in the ecclesiastical acceptation) was that of the Ebionites—Jewish converts to Christianity; forming a sect whose name offers an insurmountable difficulty to the ecclesiastical historian, since it is impossible to ascertain whether that appellation is derived from a Hebrew word which signifies a *pauper*, or from the founder of the sect. The former derivation is, however, more probable than the other. The information which we have about the doctrines of the Ebionites comes through Epiphanius, a bishop of the fifth century, a man of the most bigoted, narrow, and passionate mind. But in comparing what he says of these heretics with what is known of the ancient Jewish Gnostics, considerable light is derived, and the substance of their views may be reduced to this.

The aim of all Gnostic systems was simply to account for the existence of evil, without implicating the moral character of God. By a very absurd, yet too natural, blunder, all the Gnostics conceived that this might be accomplished by means of a system of emanations from God, which should place all imperfections at a very great distance from him. Hence the chain of generations of worlds, which they conceived as having for its lowest link man and this earth, was almost interminable. The immediate emanations from God were, of course, the highest and most perfect. As to the origin of the evil which had mixed itself with the more remote emanations, the Gnostics were divided. Some conceived an eternal and self-existent power of evil and darkness, which, having seduced some of the beings descended from God, succeeded in corrupting his creation. Others explained the imperfection and consequent evil of the lower parts of the universe as a natural degeneracy, originating in their distance from the supreme and all-perfect Being.

Among the Jewish Gnostics, who generally incorporated their theosophical systems with their national Scriptures, there were many, as the Ebionites, who asserted the existence of what may be called a MODEL MAN, a most perfect being, very nearly or immediately descended from God, who was the TYPE of perfect mankind. This SPIRITUAL MAN was originally united with Adam, but was forced to separate himself from our first parent on account of his sin. Desirous, however, of recovering our fallen race, the model man appeared united to the most holy men mentioned in the Old Testament. Finally, he fully possessed the person of

Jesus of Nazareth; and having controlled every action of his life, directing them all to the purpose of collecting the elect out of the world, deserted him on the cross. The kingdom, however, of this model man, according to these dreamers, will be a glorious one; and the true followers of Jesus will be the happy members of it, in the high regions which peculiarly belong to that pure emanation of the Divine nature.

You are probably astonished at the absurdity as well as the capriciousness of such a system, and will not easily account for the fact of its having a succession of followers for about four centuries. Such, however, is the power of whatever exists in the minds of men, as the groundwork of what may be called their philosophical notions. The highest state of intellectual refinement is necessary to prevent such notions from mixing with everything which the mind subsequently receives. I believe that, some generations after us, people will feel an astonishment similar to yours, upon learning the intimate connection which, in our days, is allowed to exist between what most Christians conceive to be saving faith and the scholastic notions of past ages. The notions of *substance,* of *properties* or *attributes,* of *natures,* of *persons,* of *matter,* of *form,* and many others which at present constitute so very important a part of the orthodox doctrines, were they not so familiar to our ears and minds, would not appear less strange than the model man and the emanations of the Gnostics. But the notions of these emanations, before the appearance of Christianity, existed in many a mind as a sublime part of science; they were a branch of the philosophy of that age, and as such they attached themselves to the Gospel, as soon as the Christians most unwisely allowed that the revelation of God through Jesus was in any way directed to inform mankind concerning the nature of the Deity and his modes of existence; the manner in which he might unite himself with an individual of the human species, and act in that individual without destroying his personality, his human will, and his human nature. When the necessity of any such kind of faith was admitted, there was no possibility of escaping philosophical corruptions, and their long train of evils. Divines found themselves compelled to choose some philosophical language, and some philosophical views, among those which were in existence: the dominant church party, on the other hand, was induced to raise some other philosophy to the dignity of Orthodoxy, degrading and persecuting all other theories as damnable heresies.

There existed but one method of avoiding these evils: to avoid the philosophy of those ages; never to make any philosophical *theory* whatever a part of the Christian doctrine. Such was the method recommended by Paul; but this method would ill accord with the ambition, the love of power and wealth, which, even in the time of the apostles (as we know from Paul's testimony*), broke out among the leaders of Christian churches. Let me again invite your attention, for a few moments, to the Gospel, without Orthodoxy, that you may see how utterly unfit it is for the purpose of worldly-minded men.

The Gospel, without Orthodoxy, is an invitation to the whole of mankind, without distinction of Jew or

---

* Νομιζόντων πορισμὸν εἶναι τὴν εὐσέβειαν; *supposing that godliness is an income.* 1st Tim. vi. 5.

Gentile, slave or freeman, to acknowledge Jesus of Nazareth as their only guide in matters concerning their souls; to receive him as the only person whom they may trust in regard to the conditions of obtaining the pardon of moral offences and the promise of happiness in a future life. This invitation was originally made by Christ himself, carried on by his immediate disciples, and intended to be continued till the end of the world, through the zeal and activity of a succession of believers in the Christ. The New Testament was (we may reasonably suppose, for as it was not authoritatively delivered, but spontaneously collected, we have no other ground for the assertion) intended by Providence to perpetuate some historical facts concerning Christ and his apostles, as also some doctrines and moral admonitions. The propagation of these documents has been left to the care of Christians; but no AUTHORITY has been bestowed on any human being to interpret these books to others. We find, in various parts of those books, a promise of individual guidance, by means of a secret influence called the SPIRIT OF CHRIST.* Of this influence it is said, that it will guide the believers *into* all the TRUTH: and, since the design of Christ's mission was the spiritual safety or SALVATION of his followers, that truth must be such a portion of the infinite truth which exists in God, as is necessary for the salvation or spiritual safety of *each individual*. We have, indeed, no authority to assert that, in such an immense variety of character and circumstances as we observe among mankind, the same identical notions and convictions are necessary in all to produce that salutary state of moral feeling, that con-

* See note at the end.

formity of the human will to the will of God (as it is made known to us by the Christ), which seems to be the essence of the Christian faith demanded in the New Testament. Under these circumstances, we may fairly compare Christianity to a moral SCHOOL opened for all mankind. The indispensable condition for admission, is the reception of the Christ as supreme MASTER concerning everything connected with religion. Whoever professes this acceptance of Christ, is a Christian. The person thus admitted to *learn*, must use his best endeavours, in the first place, to obtain by prayer (the essence of which is sincere desire—εὐχή) and purity of life the invisible guidance of the Christ or the Spirit of God: he should, in the second place, study the records called the New Testament, not as an infallible oracle, which they are evidently not, but as documents which, in spite of the human imperfections of their writers, breathe the purest Gospel spirit, and must always stand, if not as a divinely-appointed rule of everything a Christian must believe, certainly as a firm barrier against a total degeneracy of Christianity under any circumstances whatever. But every member of this spiritual school should remember that he is only a DISCIPLE, like all the rest: the school has only one MASTER,* the Christ; and to him, under God, are the pupils accountable for their progress.

If any one asks me where it is that we are to find *the Christ*, our Leader and Master, I will answer (although at present I cannot do proper justice to what I have to say), the Christ "is with us to the end of the world."

---

* One is your Master, *even* (the) Christ. Matt. xxiii. ver. 8 and 10. ὁ Χριστός, in both places.

The man Jesus, the highest representative of the Reason or Logos of God, cannot have a corporeal omnipresence: but *the Christ*, or, in other words, the Divine Reason, is within every man, in the shape of conscience, or that highest moral-intellectual faculty which the ancients called *the Leader.** The spirit of the Christ, which was without measure in Jesus, will never be absent from any man who, according to his knowledge and circumstance, will cultivate that spirit after the example of the great Prophet of Nazareth. But could such a system afford the least advantage to men who wished for rule over others? Impossible. Establish, however, the necessity of ORTHODOXY; make Christianity consist, not in sincere, internal subjection of the mind to God, but in the acceptance of some particular abstract views— views not relative to our affections and conduct, but to the *nature of things* in the invisible world, and chiefly to the nature of God himself; allow SECONDARY TEACHERS, whose decisions you are to follow either as an infallible rule or as an authority which, though not infallible, it is morally wrong to reject; and you will instantly perceive the immense power which these teachers will have over all who put themselves under them. It is true that these men will have a great number of rivals; but in proportion to their multitude and the uncertainty of their claims, will be the arbitrary value which those who expect to be saved by acquiescence in *orthodox* opinions must bestow on that standard which they choose for themselves. Now, since ORTHODOXY is a title to power, it must act upon the human mind just

* τὸ ἡγεμονικόν.

as any other instrument of ambition. Since ORTHODOXY is the bond which unites large bodies of men under the guides of that ORTHODOXY; and HETERODOXY, or HERESY, raises antagonist bodies, under rulers who are thus made dangerous rivals of the Orthodox; such a principle of union and opposition must act like opposite and rival patriotisms: yet with this important difference, that one patriotism *may* allow a certain sympathy with another; but this feeling cannot exist between two creeds. *Orthodoxy* is exclusive, and cannot grant the existence of another: its essential character is the determination to bring the whole of mankind under its own dominion. Men organized into a body as professors of Orthodoxy, will resist and avenge, to the full extent of their power, every attempt to dissolve the vital principle of their UNION.

But, like any other political body, an ORTHODOX church will readily perceive that nothing unites bodies of men so strongly as opposition to others. A state of warfare, especially with neighbours, makes patriotism a violent passion, and consolidates the union of those who fight under its banners. Hence the fact, which every page of ecclesiastical history attests, that condemnation of others is the very soul of Orthodoxy. No ORTHODOX man is satisfied that he believes his own doctrine unless he condemns from his heart every one who dissents from him. To prove the truth of this assertion beyond doubt, I have only to refer to the acts of every council and synod which has been celebrated in the Christian world. Every kind of ORTHODOXY, in fact, essentially supposes a HETERODOXY in the sense of a wrong and damnable system. But here you may observe the steps by which DISSENT was gradually made a crime, and how it was identified with practical DISSENSION—the HERESY which the Apostle Paul justly deprecates. I beg you to remark the original and etymological meaning of Heterodoxy. That word only expresses DIFFERENCE of doctrine. Like the word HERESY, its original and essential notion is DIFFERENCE. It must, therefore, be acknowledged that at the period when those two words, HERESY and HETERODOXY, began to be used by Christians, the notion that difference of doctrine is inconsistent with the spirit of Christianity, was not common and established.

But the fact, of which those very ancient ecclesiastical words still bear traces, may be positively and historically confirmed. The earliest Christian writer from whose pen we have what may properly be called a collection of literary works, is Justin the Martyr. The publication of his principal writings took place about A.D. 140. One of his most important works is a Dialogue, in which he introduces a Jew, under the name of Trypho, with whom Justin discusses, at great length, the claims of Christianity to be considered as a divine revelation. With the merits of that work we have at present nothing to do: I only mention it to prove the fact, that so late as the middle of the second century, persons who, professing that Christ had no higher nature than that of a man, received him nevertheless as the Messiah, were not supposed to have lost their baptismal claims to the name and privilege of Christians. This fact clearly appears in Justin's Dialogue. In answer to the repeated objections of the Jew against the doctrine which supposes the existence of more than one Divine person, Justin says, that even if Christians could not prove that the being who appeared as Jesus of Nazareth had not existed before he was born in the world as a man, they would only be convicted of a mistake; and adds, that this question should be entirely separated from that of Jesus being the CHRIST—the MESSIAH. "For (I translate the most important part of the passage) there are (I said), my friends,* some of us (literally some of our sort) who, confessing him to be Christ, yet declare him to be a man descended from men. With these persons I do not agree; nor would most of those who believe with me say what those persons say."† Here we find the original tone of mind which the apostles had endeavoured to produce among Christians in respect to abstract doctrines. The point to which Justin alludes is one which most divines among us consider as the very essence of Christian faith. Justin himself, with almost all his contemporary Christians of Gentile extraction, believed that Christ had existed, in a nature approaching to the divine, before he became man. But, instead of flinging curses and anathemas at the Nazarenes or the

* Trypho is represented in the Dialogue as attended by some companions.

† Καὶ γάρ εἰσί τινες, ὦ φίλοι, ἔλεγον, ἀπὸ τοῦ ἡμετέρου γένους, ... εἶναι ἄνθρωπον δὲ ἐξ ἀνθρώπων γενόμενον ἀποφαινόμενοι, οἷς οὐ συντίθεμαι, οὐδ᾽ ἂν πλεῖστοι ταὐτά μοι δοξάσαντες, εἴποιεν. (Dial. 48, Otto.) Bishop Bull contends that instead of ἡμετέρου, we ought to read ὑμετέρου. But, besides that there is not the least authority from manuscripts for this change, Justin's protest, that he does not agree with the people he mentions, shews that, without that protest, he might be supposed to agree with them, since he had described them as "some of us." Had he spoken of *Jews*, there would have been no need of this caution. Justin's argument depends entirely on the concession, that the divinity, or rather the superhuman and *godlike* nature of Christ, is not the point for which he contended as essential to Christianity, but only his being the promised Messiah.

Ebionites (it is not quite certain to which of these primitive Unitarians he alludes), he modestly expresses his dissent from them, without, however, questioning their Christianity. No doctrine concerning the nature of things, either in God or in man, was as yet supposed to be a part of the Gospel. The surrender of the will to the will of God through the Christ, the hope of salvation under his guidance—such were, in the opinion of the best Christians, down to the middle of the second century, the only conditions of Christian fellowship.

This tolerant and charitable temper had, indeed, nearly disappeared about one hundred years after Justin; but it was not absolutely extinct. The pious, the learned, though mystical and fanciful Origen,* has recorded his regret at the intolerance which was already prevalent in his time. In allusion to the Ebionites, a Christian sect of whose real character and doctrines (as it constantly happens in ecclesiastical history) we can know nothing with certainty, except that, to the Orthodox party, they were an object of the most violent and unqualified abuse, Origen has a remarkable passage. Having related the affecting history of the blind man near Jericho, who, in spite of the threatenings of the multitude, persevered in his prayer for sight till he obtained that boon from Jesus, Origen compares the Ebionite Unitarians to the blind man, and the Gentile Christians (who were then approaching to the notions to which the Council of Nice, supported by imperial power, gave ascendency) to the multitude who would not allow the blind to implore the mercy of the Saviour. "Never-

---

* Flourished about A.D. 230.

theless (says Origen), although the multitudes command him to be silent, he cries much the more, because he believed in Jesus, though he believed in him rather humanly,* and in a loud voice says to him, 'Jesus, thou Son of David, have mercy on me.'" In this truly modest and tolerant spirit were the Ebionites of his time treated by the profoundly learned, excellent, and cruelly persecuted Origen. "How different (observes the pious TRINITARIAN Neander, marking his own words for emphasis), how totally different many things would have been if men had, in this spirit of love and liberty, allowed free course to the grace of the Saviour over all who call upon him; if they had considered the various points of view of the Christian progress towards the ripeness of manhood in the faith; and had not determined to reduce by force the various kinds of minds to one and the same measure!"†

But a totally opposite spirit had already obtained ascendency among Christians. The presidents of congregations who had monopolized the title of Bishops, formerly common to all Presbyters, were now fully aware of the importance of establishing the exclusive claims of one party, against all others, to be considered

---

* πιστεύων μὲν ἐπὶ τὸν 'Ιησοῦν, ἀνθρωπικώτερον δὲ πιστεύων. It is this identical notion, that to believe Christ's nature to be only *human*, is to form a *low* conception of him—it is this explaining the Scriptures according to *sentiment*, which has made, in all ages, the Athanasian interpretation so popular. The whole passage of Origen is to be found in his Commentary on Matthew, Part xvi. Vol. III. pp. 773 and 774. *Paris*, ed. *Delarue*. (Migne, Vol. III. p. 1413.)

† Neander, *Geschichte*, Vol. I. Part ii. page 408. He adds, that Origen was aware of the fact that the Ebionites, whose prejudices were thoroughly Jewish, condemned the Apostle Paul as a corrupter of the gospel. Yet Origen did not reject those men as necessarily unchristian!

as the sole possessors and distributors of *genuine Christianity*. Forming a united body, upon the plan of the political confederacies of the Greeks, the majority of the Christian Bishops became a most tyrannical aristocracy. The love of power and of gain combined with their very general narrow-mindedness, ignorance, and intolerance, in transforming those passions which, for the sake of distinction from the animal appetites, might well be called the SPIRITUAL PASSIONS, into the highest and most important virtues. ORTHODOXY, *i.e.* the spurious philosophical notions which this confederacy had adopted in connection with the Gospel, was made essential to Christianity. Whoever did not hold the same views, was declared an enemy of Christ and religion; and as the confederacy extended itself over the face of the Roman empire, the unfortunate being who incurred the condemnation of his Bishop in some obscure town of a semi-barbarous corner of the Roman territory, was regularly hunted down by all the orthodox associates, till, as it actually happened to multitudes in later times, he was forced either to submit, or to take refuge among the barbarous nations, who in such cases were always found more charitable and humane than the Christian clergy. Thus ORTHODOXY converted the religion of love and charity into a source of some of the worst evils which have oppressed mankind, and which even the rapid progress of knowledge in our own days seems still unable totally to subdue.

LETTER V.

ON THE PRIDE OF REASON.

"Je vous applaudis fort lorsque vous voulez que la foi soit fondée en raison ; sans cela, pourquoi préférerions-nous la Bible à l'Alcoran ou aux anciens livres des Bramines ? Aussi nos théologiens et autres savans hommes l'ont-ils reconnu, et c'est ce qui nous a fait avoir de si beaux ouvrages de la vérité de la religion Chrétienne, et tant de belles preuves qu'on a mises en avant contre les païens et autres mécréans anciens et modernes. Aussi les personnes sages ont toujours tenu pour suspects ceux qui ont prétendu qu'il ne fallait point se mettre en peine des raisons et preuves quand il s'agit de croire ; chose impossible, en effet, *à moins que croire signifie réciter ou répéter et laisser passer sans s'en mettre en peine, comme font bien des gens, et comme c'est même le caractère de quelques nations plus que d'autres.*"—*Leibnitz, Nouveaux Essais* (l. iv. c. 17): quoted by *Victor Cousin, Hist. de la Philosophie,* T. II. p. 474.

My dear Friend,

The notion of Orthodoxy, among Protestants, like some hotly hunted debtors, has been obliged to leave its pursuers at fault, by crossing into another jurisdictional district. Orthodoxy, finding itself unsafe in the domains of argument, flies towards those of moral sentiment; and just at the moment when it might be expected to surrender, it turns sharply round, and bodily charges REASON with SIN. This is an alarming change. Before this moral discovery, we exerted our reason to the utmost of our power, confident that we had no spiritual danger to fear: now, most unfortunately, we are made to suspect that our sin may be great in proportion to the power of our arguments. What, indeed, in common language, we call PRIDE, is usually connected with *power;* and the existence of the latter is, for most people, a pretty strong presumption of the presence of the former. It must therefore happen, that when reason is accused of pride, the charge will appear already more than half-substantiated, if reason has been too hard for the opponents. Power of any kind, unless it can reward and punish to a certain degree, is not an enviable possession. I have no doubt that if a *sin*, to be called PRIDE OF SIGHT, had been as necessary to some influential class as the PRIDE OF REASON is to the orthodox parties all over the world, every sharp-sighted man, who wished to live in peace and avoid the scandal of discovering things which his neighbours either could not or would not see, would now be obliged to wear spectacles.

PRIDE OF REASON! What can it be? I confess that, having for a long time been honestly endeavouring to find out the exact meaning of that phrase, as applied in theological controversy, I have not yet quite deciphered it. It might be expected that those who use it would explain it; but they will not take that trouble. I shall therefore be obliged to try what I can do in making out what they mean.

PRIDE is a vice: no one who uses that word doubts it. But what does it consist in? Few stop to ascertain that point. I go, in the first place, to Cruden's Concordance, a book remarkable for definitions or descriptions of important words frequently used in the Scriptures, and am disappointed to find none. But, fortunately, Dr. Johnson gives no less than *seven* meanings of the word.

Out of this number, however, only *two*, as implying something *wrong*, can be of service in my present inquiry:

1st. "Inordinate and unreasonable self-esteem."

2nd. "Insolence, rude treatment of others; insolent exultation."

We will, if you please, treasure up these two explanations of the great lexicographer.

I have laid it down as unquestionable, that *pride* means *a vice;* and I find a proof of the *unfavourable* signification of the word in the established phrase, *honest* pride. If *pride* did not essentially signify something wrong and vicious, it would not be necessary to qualify it, in certain cases, by means of the addition, *honest*. The existence of such a phrase as the one last mentioned, clearly shews that there is a human sentiment which has no proper name in English (I do not recollect any modern language that possesses it), and which is expressed by that of a *vice*, modified by another word which signifies something virtuous. What, then, is that sentiment? What do we mean by *honest pride?* I believe these words signify *consciousness of worth*, or *dignity of mind*, free from presumption above others. There is nothing vicious in this feeling; on the contrary, it is acknowledged (except by those extravagant ascetics who make a sense of degradation essential to Christianity) to be the purest natural source and support of a virtuous conduct.* How is it, then, that *pride*, which

---

* *Self-respect*, a feeling which becomes *honest pride* when it is insulted, and has to assert its rights against the unfeelingness or injustice of others, is respect for the voice of *Reason*, which every sincere and honest man considers as the voice of God, always ready to speak when reverently consulted within the sanctuary of our CONSCIENCE.

(if we consider some of its significations, as splendour, dignity) seems, originally, not to have expressed anything *inordinate*, has been so universally and irrevocably fixed to signify *excess?* I think I can explain this fact. The *self-esteem* of every individual has a natural rival in that of every other. Hence the invidiousness of self-commendation. Every one knows, by constant experience, what a rare combination of circumstances must take place, and with what a delicate hand those circumstances must be managed, in order to make self-commendation endurable. As words are not the only signs of what passes in the mind, the habitual sense of personal *worth* and *respectability* is universally perceived through the whole manner of the person who has it. This perception is quickened by the self-esteem of the observer; and as the self-esteem of each person may be said to occupy a certain space, it invariably limits that to which others would gladly extend their own. Though this language is, of course, figurative, every one who has attentively observed mankind will grant that there are individuals who have a most real though inexplicable power of making others shrink into very limited dimensions. Those who possess that power must naturally become objects of a very general dislike. Besides, it seldom happens that two men, being placed in constant juxta-position, do not, in a certain degree, *crowd* each other. Sometimes they find themselves obliged to part company; but more frequently they mould, shape, and *pack* the two *self-esteems*, like travellers in a narrow carriage. But in this process, as well as in that of the illustration, the allotment of space is never equal; and the weak and sensitive will always be compelled to shrink more and more, and fret secretly at the bulky and unyielding dimensions of his neighbour.

It is, therefore, evident that every *self-esteem* is a *claim*, and sometimes a *power*, over all others ; and *claims* (of *powers* we need not speak) however just, especially if they are incessant, are seldom or never acknowledged without a certain degree of displeasure. Add to this natural feeling, which good men subdue, one which, as (in a variable degree) it is perfectly just, no man should endeavour to destroy in himself, or he would lower his character to that of a slave—I speak of a proper watchfulness against the *encroachments*, the *inordinate* claims, of other men's self-esteem. There must consequently exist an almost general uneasiness on this subject. Great love and pure friendship will certainly remove this state of watchfulness and constant suspicion. But those two blessings are rare. Society proceeds, however, pretty smoothly by the practical good sense which teaches its more refined members (though these are the class whose self-esteem is most sensitive) how to avoid clashing with each other. In fact, *fashionable refinement* may be defined, the art of condensing our self-esteem within ourselves, and shewing it just enough to have it understood that we will not give much more room for the self-esteem of others.

And here we have the answer to the question why *pride*, in its unfavourable sense, has an established verbal sign in all languages, while they want a proper name for the virtuous feeling of which *pride* is an excess. In the daily difficulty of social life above described, in this perpetual jealousy, this unavoidable rivalry, every one stands continually in the character of *judge and party.* Partiality in judging other men's self-esteem is, therefore, almost unavoidable; consequently we are very seldom in want of the name of the *virtue,* except to apply it to ourselves, and then we scarcely dare use it. The word, therefore, which originally in all languages had probably a favourable signification, becomes inevitably, in the course of time, a name for the *excess* which every man finds in all others.*

It must now be evident that all I have said of *pride* must apply to that word when combined with the word *reason.* As that phrase is invariably used to convey reproach, we may proceed in our examination by substituting for the word *pride* Dr. Johnson's first definition, with such changes only as grammar absolutely requires in the combination. *Pride of* REASON will, therefore, be *an immoderate esteem of one's own reason.* A man who values his own reason immoderately, or beyond the proper measure, is guilty of *pride of reason.* Our next step in the inquiry must be to find the *proper measure* beyond which we ought not to esteem our reason. Here the analogy of the first definition may guide us. We may justly be charged with excess of *self-esteem* when we invade the proper self-esteem of others. In the same manner, a man is to be blamed for PRIDE OF REASON *when the value he sets upon his own share of that gift induces him to invade the share of another man.* This is an *inordinate* esteem of *reason* as he possesses it individually.

* The Germans still preserve the word *stolz* in a favourable sense, though it is frequently used for *Uebermuth,* shewing the general tendency. See *Krug's Lexikon,* under *Hochmuth.*

I do not see what valid objection can be made to this statement. I am aware that the phrase, *pride of reason*, is not unfrequently employed to express something like a rebellion of reason against God, the supreme Fountain of Reason. But the idea is too absurd to deserve a moment's attention. Any one who could oppose his own reason to the Infinite Source of mind and intelligence, would be a madman. Such an intention has never crossed the mind of any man in his senses. Every man knows more or less, as it were instinctively, that when he speaks of his own reason, he wishes to express nothing but his perception of one and the same *universal reason*, peculiar to no individual, but supreme over all. This is God.* The source of the notion which supposes this resistance of the human reason to God, lies in the gross mistake of imagining that any revelation from God

---

* *Fénélon, Existence de Dieu*, prem. part, chap. iv., de la *Raison de l'Homme* :—

"A la vérité, ma raison est en moi ; car il faut que je rentre sans cesse en moi-même pour la trouver : mais la raison supérieure qui me corrige dans le besoin, et que je consulte, n'est point à moi, et elle ne fait point partie de moi-même. . . . Ainsi, ce qui paraît le plus à nous et être le fond de nous-mêmes, je veux dire notre raison, est ce qui nous est le moins propre et qu'on doit croire le plus emprunté. Nous recevons sans cesse et à tout moment une raison supérieure à nous, comme nous respirons sans cesse l'air qui est un corps étranger, ou comme nous voyons sans cesse tous les objects voisins de nous à la lumière du soleil, dont les rayons sont des corps étrangers a nos yeux.† . . . Il y a une école intérieure où l'homme reçoit ce qu'il ne peut ni se donner ni attendre des autres hommes, qui vivent d'emprunt comme lui. . . Où est-elle cette raison parfaite qui est si près de moi et si différente de moi ? . . . . Où est-elle cette raison suprême ? N'est elle pas le Dieu que je cherche ?"—*Quoted by Cousin*, ubi sup. p. 479, *note*. Independently of controversy, I am persuaded that λόγος, in the first chapter of St. John's Gospel, is the *Supreme Reason* personified by a figure of speech.

† See note to this page at the end.

can exist for a rational being like man, except through that partial perception of the supreme reason which individuals enjoy in various degrees. This is what we call *our* reason. Among that class of Christians who accuse others of deliberately opposing their own reason to the revelations of God, there cannot be one who has ever considered that when he himself receives anything as revealed in Scripture, he is only following the dictates of his *reason*. He may believe (as is not unfrequently the case) the greatest absurdities; he may embrace what, upon any other subject, he would reject as a palpable contradiction; nevertheless, he does all this because he finds some *more general reason* for sacrificing his reason on these particulars. He grounds that more general reason on God, the eternal Source of reason; and he does well. But he should, at the same time, perceive that he is not sacrificing his own reason to God,—a sacrifice which to the supreme reason would be abominable, but an inferior and partial judgment of his own reason for the sake of another which appears to him more sound and comprehensive. Exactly the same is the case of every *sincere* man who rejects what others embrace as God's word. He does not deny that *word;* he only denies either the testimony or the judgment of other men. It cannot, indeed, be conceived that any man in his sound mind, believing that any, even the most incomprehensible mystery, has been actually communicated by God to man, nevertheless refuses to acknowledge it, accusing God either of error or falsehood. This is impossible. To believe in God, and at the same time to make his reason inferior to human reason, is a contradiction which cannot lay hold on our mind. Human reason has never opposed the divine and supreme reason, knowing that it did so: it is only the human will, that, in spite of reason, has the power, and indeed a very decided propensity, to oppose the will of God. No man who understands what he says, will talk of reason's rebellion against God.—But let us return to our subject.

Having found that *pride of reason* is *an aggression upon other men's reason*, arising from an over-estimate of the worth of the aggressor's own, we may now proceed in our inquiry, Who are justly chargeable with pride of *reason?* Is it those who, having examined the Scriptures, propose their own collective sense of those books to the acceptance of others, but blame them not for rejecting it? or those who positively assert that their own sense of the Scriptures is the only one which an honest man, not under diabolical delusion, can find there? The answer is so plain, that a child who could understand the terms of the question might give it. And yet experience has taught me that there is no chance of unravelling the confused ideas which prevent many a well-meaning Christian from perceiving that the charge of pride of reason falls upon the Orthodox. Their own *sense* of the Scriptures (such is the dizzy whirl which their excited feelings produce) must be the *word of God*, because THEY cannot find another. *My sense* of the Scripture (for instance) must, on the contrary, be a damnable error, because it is the work of my *reason*, which opposes the Word of God, *i.e.* THEIR sense of the Scriptures: hence the conclusion that I am guilty of *pride of reason.* "Renounce that *pride* (they say), and you will see in the Scriptures what we propose to you :" which is to say, *Surrender your reason to ours, and you will agree with us.*

I have already, incidentally, illustrated the theological notion of *pride of reason* by what (if the same interests, internal and external, which occasion this clamour against reason were involved) would certainly have been called the *pride of sight.* Allow me to dwell, once more, on the nature of that very considerable *vice. Pride of sight* would be defined, an *inordinate value set on the individual's power of vision.* The most approved and meritorious method to avoid this criminal excess would be, to put out one's eyes. The person who had performed this noble act of self-denial should be entitled to declare, uncontradicted, that he never before had seen so well. He should, in consequence of the superiority of this new sight, be chosen leader of other men who still kept those delusive organs, *the eyes.** The sacrifice of the eyes would be offered up as a testimony of reverence to the Creator of Light, as that of reason is now considered an appropriate tribute to the Fountain of it. Of two men who looked, apparently with the same intensity, at a remote and indistinct object, *he* who asserted that he saw even the minutest parts, and denied the possibility that any good and honest person could differ from himself in the description, should be declared *thereby* to possess the virtue of *humbleness of sight :* he, on the contrary, who confessed that his eyes could not discover what the other man said he saw, but granted that he might be allowed to enjoy his view without

* Il est vrai que de notre temps une personne de la plus grande élévation disait, qu'en articles de foi, il fallait se crever les yeux pour voir clair.—*Leibnitz, Nouveaux Essais,* quoted by *Victor Cousin.*

blame, should be charged with *pride of sight* in a most offensive degree. Though both were exerting their power of vision under the light of the same sun, and had their eyes equally open, the latter should be accused of despising and hating the light of heaven, and be strongly suspected of *winking:* if this could not be proved externally, it should be firmly believed that he had an internal power of paralyzing his optic nerve, and making himself stone-blind. The happy observer of such parts of the remote object as he in the same breath declared to be *invisible*,* should earnestly call upon the other, as if he would save him from death and infamy, to renounce his *pride of sight*, and agree to *see* the same things which he (the adviser) had, in his great *humility of vision*, firmly determined to discover. Such should be the moral law of the PRIDE OF SIGHT.

I confess to you, my dear friend, that, when combating such pitiable delusions as occur at every step in theological controversy, I have often felt a despondency which tempted me to throw away the pen, never to employ it again upon such subjects. Nothing, indeed, but my deep-felt conviction of the enormous evils which intolerance, in this its last disguise, is producing in the world, has supported my determination to oppose it to my last breath. Among the hopeless cases of that fever of religious feeling which creates a lamentable confusion of thought upon these subjects, there may be patients who possess natural candour and intellectual strength sufficient to extricate them, I do not say from

---

* Thus the Deity is declared to be *incomprehensible* in the minutest description of his *mode of being* that ever was attempted in human language.

the *doctrines* of Orthodoxy,—for that is to me a minor point,—but from the mischievous error of taking their own *sense* of Scripture for the word of God itself; and from the *essentially intolerant* belief that any man who opposes that sense is betrayed by his *pride of reason* into rebellion against God.

Will any candid and reasonable man deny that *articles of religion,* or creeds, are only explanations of Scripture? I ask, are these *explanations* the work of *reason*, or the result of *inspiration?*—My question is addressed exclusively to Protestants; for it is *their* inconsistent and contradictory intolerance which I am opposing. That of the Roman Catholics must be opposed by disproving the inspiration of their authoritative expounder —whether the Church, or the Pope, or both. But the Protestants have no alternative: either they must admit that the exposition of the Scriptures given in their respective creeds is a work of reason, or they must embrace the Popish principle of infallibility. That kind of unauthoritative tradition to which some Protestant writers had fondly clung,* especially in the Church of England, makes not the least difference. To ascertain that tradition, is a work of reason assisted by learning; and the most successful search of the views and opinions of ancient days in some churches, can give to the result no higher character than that of a very questionable historical probability. But if, in the formation of all creeds whatever, the reason of the framers, as employed in finding the *sense* of Scripture, is the ultimate

* See a *Discourse on Unauthoritative Tradition;* a very able work of Dr. Hawkins, Provost of Oriel College, Oxford.

I

support, the real foundation upon which their articles stand, what instance of *pride of reason* can be more glaring than that of attributing some kind of guilt to the rejection of that purely human commentary on the Bible? Whether few or many men combined for the purpose of passing the work of their reason for the only true sense of the Scripture,—thus encroaching upon the rights of other men's reason,—can make no difference, unless it be that of aggravating their guilt. If many combine to do an unjust and illegal act, they are guilty, not only of the individual wrong committed, but add to it that of conspiracy. Let all the bishops and priests in the world unite to awe other men's reason into submission to the inferences which the *council* (as such assemblies have been called) suppose they have drawn from the Scripture; their multitude only shews that the *pride* of THEIR *reason* is attended by a consciousness of its *weakness*. *Reason* does not derive strength from crowds. The reason of the most obscure individual, b it but true *reason*, is sufficient to subdue the world, if fairly left to take its course.

It is remarkable that Christians are accused of *pride of reason* in proportion as their view of Christianity contains fewer *doctrines of inference* than that of the accusers. Compare the creed of the Trinitarian with that of the Unitarian. The former may be true, and the latter erroneous, though I adhere to the latter; but, unquestionably, the *Trinitarian creed* is nearly made up of *inferences*—it is almost entirely a work of *reason*, though, in my opinion, sadly misapplied. Why, then, is the *Unitarian* accused of *pride of reason* when he only employs it to shew that the Trinitarian has not any *sound reason* to draw those inferences? Which of the two is guilty of encroaching upon another man's *rights of reason?* Is it not he who claims for his inferences—the work of his own *reason*—an authority above human *reason?*

Is it not, however, to *inferences* alone (the work of logical reason) that the Trinitarian creed owes its existence, and, more than its existence, its popularity? My observation has shewn me, and that of every competent judge will find, that the strongest hold which that creed has on the minds of its supporters, consists in *preconceived theories* concerning the nature of God and of sin, and of some *necessity* which places the Divine Nature in a state of difficulty in regard to the pardon of sin. The work of saving the race of man from a most horrible fate depends (according to this theory) not only on a very mysterious method of overcoming the difficulty which prevents pardon by an act of mercy on repentance, but also on the acknowledgment of the *mystery* by the sinner. The remedy prepared by the wisdom of God is (according to this theory) totally powerless, unless we believe a certain explanation of the *manner* in which it acts. Now, people who cordially embrace this view very naturally work themselves into a state of the most agonizing excitement: for if the whole world is to perish because it does not know how the saving remedy acts, or because its activity is explained in a wrong way, benevolent men, who think themselves in possession of that important secret, must burn with zeal to spread it, and with indignation against those who propagate an explanation which deprives the remedy of all its power. "Believing," says an *orthodox* writer,* though a dissenter from the *Orthodoxy* of the Church of England, "the doctrine (of the divinity of Christ) to comprehend within itself the hopes of a guilty and perishing world, while I would contend *meekly*, I must be pardoned if at the same time I contend earnestly." It is this preconceived theory (one of the strangest that was ever founded on reasonings *à priori*) that guides most Christians in the exposition of the New Testament, and even in that of many passages of the Hebrew Scriptures. The notion that sin *could not* be pardoned unless a person *equal to God* suffered for it, is the deeply-coloured glass through which the Orthodox read the Scriptures. I do not *blame* them for this extraordinary conception. What I earnestly wish is, that their religious fears may allow them to perceive that this theory of redemption is made up of *preconceived notions and inferences.* Even if that theory were true, it would be unquestionably a work of *reason* working by inference. Can, then, the attempt to make it the very soul of the Gospel be acquitted of the charge which is constantly in the mouth of the Orthodox? Are they not guilty of the *pride of reason?*

But here the *Orthodox* (I mean the man who considers all that dissent from him *necessarily* in error) escapes again into the mist of ideas which hovers always at hand in the field of theological controversy. That the multitude will follow him into the darkness is natural and certain. Reluctance to believe what is directly against the first principles of reason, appears to the mass of unthinking Christians as intellectual pride.

* Mr. Wardlaw, quoted by the Rev. Mr. Yates in his *Vindication of Unitarianism*, p. 41, *American edit.*

Readiness to believe what cannot even be propounded in uncontradictory words, is the purest faith. Considering this popular feeling, if two views of Christianity, the Athanasian and the Unitarian, are brought before that mass of Christians who have been assiduously taught that the efficacy of faith (as it is vulgarly supposed of medicines) is proved by the offensiveness of what is to be believed, nobody can doubt to which they will give the preference. The Unitarian creed will be rejected, upon the ground that it raises no dislike or reluctance; the other will be embraced, because it produces the expected effect of faith. *Credo quia impossibile.* The plain Christian who entertains these notions (and those who are educated according to the Orthodox system entertain them in proportion to their want of intellectual activity) cannot fail to discover the clearest proofs of *pride of reason* in a view of Christianity which does not bewilder him; for if it were not the work of that *pride* (he will say), how could it be so agreeable to *reason*—so *reasonable?*

I would, however, earnestly recommend to persons of this description to examine whether, in point of *reasonableness*, the New Testament (take it all in all) is not more in agreement with *reason*, with the plain Unitarian statement, than with the complicated creeds of the Orthodox churches? I do not speak of three or four texts (excluding the evident *interpolations*, which, curiously enough, are *all on the Trinitarian side);* for those texts, owing to our early imbibed notions, create at first sight some perplexity: I speak of the tone of instruction which prevails in those writings. Let the impartial inquirer observe the absence of all metaphysical specu lation in the Gospels, and compare it with abundance of scholastic philosophy in the Orthodox confessions. Let him remark, that the New Testament presupposes no previous knowledge in the persons whom the authors addressed; for those holy men well knew that they were sent principally to preach the Gospel to the poor and uneducated. On the other hand, let him reflect on the mass of strange ideas which are necessary as a *preparation* in order to understand the mere statements of the Athanasian Creed, the Confession of Augsburg, or the Thirty-nine Articles—in a word, the whole of the patristico-scholastic theology which is taught in this country. Allow me to make a brief enumeration of the previous notions which, if the New Testament were intended to convey the Orthodox system of divinity, it would necessarily presume to exist in every person to whom it is addressed by Providence. Under the name of *Orthodox*, I embrace both Arminians and Calvinists, because both are allowed admission into the Church of England; and the latter claim the privilege of Orthodoxy, I believe *exclusively*, in the Kirk of Scotland.

To be prepared for the established and orthodox sense of the New Testament, young minds must be accustomed to form to themselves the idea of a Creator—God the Father; an infinitely powerful Being, whose prominent attribute is severity; who created mankind, according to some divines *knowing*, according to others *predetermining*, that by far the greater part of all the future generations of men should, after a short mortal life, be eternally alive in torments. The opening mind must also be accustomed to consider it reasonable and just that, *because* the first parent of mankind disobeyed a precept of God concerning a certain fruit which he was not to taste, all his descendants to the remotest posterity should not only suffer diseases and death, but be born also *guilty* of *sin*, objects of *wrath* to God, morally degraded, and very far or totally removed from rectitude. Another elementary notion, not unlike this, must be instilled into the young mind in respect to Divine equity. The child must learn that since by Adam's sin all his posterity were doomed to spiritual *death* (which he must understand in the sense of *eternal life in misery*), God the Father could not consistently with his *justice* pardon them, unless some one suffered in their stead. He therefore doomed his only-begotten Son, a perfectly innocent being, equal to himself, to death. The child might be inclined to expect that, as Adam's sin involved all mankind in ruin, independently of their will, this remedy by its intrinsic power would also save ALL MEN, and finally lead them to happiness. But he must be checked in this bold use of his reason, and taught to believe that the infinite remedy prepared by God falls widely short of the extent of the evil produced by man's original disobedience.

Another previous notion of great importance, if the child is to find the Orthodox system in the New Testament, is that of an *unity* which is not *unity;* for he will certainly read repeated assertions in the Bible that God is ONE; yet by *one* he must understand *three* infinite Minds, all equally God, and nevertheless not making up *three* Gods. To proceed: the understanding has original and indestructible laws, which begin to direct it at a very early age, especially if called into activity by instruction. A quick child, though not acquainted with logic, will very soon be practically aware of one of the first principles of thought—*that*, namely, which rejects the assertion that one thing *substantially* conceived, is another thing conceived in the same manner. He will perceive the absurdity of saying that *Edward is John*, or the *horse is the cow*.* As the young pupil must be prepared to infer from the New Testament that a *perfect man* is *perfect God*, he must be carefully instructed to discard the mental principle which would represent this as a contradiction, of the same kind as it would be to say that there may be a triangle which is also a circle; perfect gold which is perfect silver; a perfect horse which is a perfect eagle, &c. &c. : or (which is commonly the case) must be imperceptibly led to consider the word God as expressing a quality, or an aggregate of qualities, which may be predicated of more than one, as the name of a species; just as we say John is man, Peter is man, Andrew is man. This latter notion is a necessary result of placing the mind between the two *logically* contradictory assertions, there is but *one* God, and there are *three* who are God. And so it is that, with the exception of a few who in this country are still acquainted with that ingeniously perverse system of words by means of which the truly *scholastic* Trinitarians (such as Bishop Bull and Waterland, who had accurately studied the fathers and schoolmen) *appear* to evade the logical contradictions with which the doctrine of the Trinity abounds—all, as I have observed for many years, take the word *God*, in regard to Jesus, as the name of a species, and more frequently of a dignity.

---

* *Res de Re prædicari non potest:* Abelard's celebrated principle, by which he confuted the Realists.

HERESY AND ORTHODOXY.

This appears in the method very frequently used to prove the divinity of Jesus, by a collection of passages in which (as the writers imagine) all the attributes of Deity are predicated of him. The whole, indeed, of their language implies something *conferred* upon the human nature of Jesus; and so far they are proceeding on a truly scriptural principle; for Jesus himself has declared that everything he possesses has been *given* to him. Thus these very pious, but not very logical men, establish quite the opposite of what they intend to prove. Deity *communicated* is a contradictory idea to that of *proper Deity*. Many, indeed, among the Trinitarians, if they understood themselves, would perceive that they only differ in *language* from some Unitarians; for I am convinced that many individuals of this denomination would give to Jesus the name of *God* in the sense of the *highest dignity* ever conferred upon an individual of the human species, if the example of Jesus himself did not teach them that there is a danger in such a stretch of language, and that it has a tendency directly opposed to the important belief in the Divine *Unity*. It is worthy of attention, that when Jesus was about to be stoned for having used language which the Jews took to mean *equality* with God, though he asserted that the application, in an improper sense, of the name *God* to men was not *blasphemy*, he still would not claim it for himself, but used the denomination, *Son of God*, in the Jewish sense of Messiah, the anointed or sanctified of God.*

---

* See John x. 29—36. It has been observed by one of the most powerful writers in the English language (Archbishop Whately), in answer to those who assert that when our Saviour said to Pilate, "My kingdom is

It is not to be expected, however, that in the process of instilling the necessary previous notions which the New Testament would require in order to convey the orthodox sense, this *collateral* mistake of supposing that the idea of God can be attributed to another being, as a conferred dignity, should be carefully opposed. The assistance of that notion in keeping up the popularity of Trinitarianism is too evident not to be *instinctively* treated with lenity, even by the very few who in this country are aware of its theological inaccuracy. The body of orthodox Christians are entirely supported in their profession of the Divinity of Jesus by the feeling that to deny it is to *degrade* the Saviour. To deprive of his *Deity* the most amiable as well as most venerable person ever known to the world, appears in the light of the greatest ingratitude. It is this feeling that erases from the mind whatever impression the voice of *Reason*, supported by the Scriptures, may have made in favour of that supreme religious truth, the Unity of God.*
The *Father* (let every one ask his own consciousness as

not of this world," he only alluded to the then present state of his kingdom, that such a view attributes to Christ a most unworthy mental reservation. Apply the same remark to Christ's answer to the Jews, and if he knew that he was *God*, and intended that such a belief should, at a future time, be made a fundamental doctrine of his religion, his answer would be such an evasion as every man who loves and reveres Jesus of Nazareth would not on any account attribute to him.

* In the interminable confusion of primitive ideas and language upon which the common acceptance of the Trinitarian doctrine reposes, people do not perceive a most simple, and in itself obvious truth, which might allay this fear of *degrading* Jesus. If Jesus be *God*, he must be that *one* God for whose exclusive honour the Unitarian contends. Jesus, in that case, can neither be degraded nor offended. But if he be *not* God, the danger of offending both the Father and him is one which a pious mind should not overlook.

well as his observation), the *Father* among us is not an object of *affection:* in regard to his incommunicable honour, the mass of Christians have no quick or delicate feeling. And is it possible to avoid this direct result of the descriptions which divines give of the Supreme God? Is he not represented as ready to destroy the world—as a *consuming fire,* that would readily devour us, if it had not spent its wrath upon the Son?* The consequence of this teaching is visible everywhere: the SON is preferred to the Father; to that Father whom Christ worshipped and loved; to that Father, for whose glory he lived and died; to that Father, to do whose will was his meat and drink. Yet Christians are now satisfied that the most certain way to secure the salvation proclaimed by Christ is to neglect "God our Saviour," and place his Son, not at God's "right hand," but occupying God's throne. A single step in the same course of feeling, assisted externally by circumstances, may land a child thus instructed upon the notion of a still milder and more accessible sort of deity—the Virgin *Mother of God*—so strong is the tendency of mankind to worship gods like unto themselves.

I believe I have omitted many of the notions which regularly prepare the minds of every rising generation, that they may not be struck with the difference between

---

* "Have you informed him (said an anxious divine to the mother of a dying boy) that God, without Christ, is a consuming, devouring fire?" Upon the acceptance of this view by the child depended his salvation, according to this Christian instructor. To what kind of heads and tempers will Christianity be confined in the course of a few generations, if it have such men for its publishers and ministers? I relate the above fact upon unquestionable authority. It took place in Dublin not long ago.

the simplicity of the New Testament and the abstruse and fanciful philosophy of the established theological systems. But what I have laid before you is more than sufficient to shew that the *rashness* (if not the *pride*) of Reason is all on the side of the Orthodox. We are, nevertheless, assured with the greatest confidence, that the entire system, of which I have given you a few specimens, is so plainly contained in the New Testament, that *he that runs may read it.*

It has cost me no small trouble to avoid in what I have been writing, even the most slight appearance of satire; yet such is the nature of everything which contradicts the first principles of *Reason*, that if you divest it of the mysterious language in which the mind has been accustomed to revere it, no care whatever can prevent the revulsion of feeling which the naked absurdity will produce. It is exactly like what I have seen in Spain in regard to the most revered objects. The *miraculous* image of the Virgin Mary, for whose honour the kings of Spain maintain, at the expense of the country, a body of dignified clergy, has its splendid dress changed once a year, *behind a large thick veil;* because even the blindest enthusiasts are aware that if the wooden frame covered with canvas which lies underneath the gems and brocade were to be seen, public adoration might in a short time end in general laughter.

But as it is the invariable custom of idol-guardians to interpret everything said of the *idol* as if it were intended against the object which (though perhaps sacred in itself) it misrepresents and distorts, so we see the framers and supporters of fanciful *inferences* from the

Scriptures constantly identifying those *inferences*, not only with the Scriptures, but with God himself. If any one treats the *contradictions* of the Athanasian Creed as he would any others expressed in language (for *contradictions* cannot exist except *in language*), he is directly accused of impiety. He is told that he is treating the most sacred things irreverently; as if the observations applied to the objects, and not to the language which misrepresents those objects. It is in this manner that a Roman Catholic multitude would say that you were laughing at Mary the Mother of *God*, if they observed you casting a look of disgust and pity at the clumsy wooden frame, with varnished head and hands, before which the attendant priests are obliged to kneel, holding lighted wax candles. In like manner, the metaphysical *inferences* which the *Reason* of the Orthodox has (as they imagine) collected from the Bible, are most positively identified with the WORD OF GOD. How, then, can we be surprised at the readiness with which the unthinking multitudes of all ranks seize the notion that the *Unitarians* set up their *Reason* above the word of God, and by the most guilty and impious intellectual pride refuse their assent to all divine MYSTERIES?

Admirably as this subject of *Mystery* has been treated by some enlightened and truly philosophical divines,* I cannot help thinking that there is still a very essential mistake to be removed concerning it. "There are mysteries in everything around us," is constantly and emphatically repeated. But I do not remember to have seen it observed anywhere, that the application of this

* See, especially, *Yates's Vindication of Unitarianism*, c. iv. part i.

fact, as an antecedent reason for believing in the mysteries of Orthodox divinity, is a fallacy. In respect to the demanded submission, there is no similarity between the *mysteries* which surround us in nature and those concerning which the Christian world has been in agitation for about eighteen centuries. The mysteries of nature stand before us, a matter of indubitable experience. We see all bodies drawn towards the centre of the earth; and the *fact* forces itself upon the credence of every individual, though we are in the dark as to the *cause* of gravitation. We see the effects of electricity and galvanism, though we are unable to trace those effects higher up in the chain of causes and effects. The cause in all such cases is *mysterious*; but the *facts* are so permanent, that we can reduce them to general laws. But, in the name of common sense, I ask, do the mysteries of the Trinity and Original Sin stand before us in the same manner? Do they even stand (as they easily might) in *express terms* in the Scriptures? When a *fact* which may be verified as often as we please presents itself in nature, *Reason* is never tempted to raise the least objection. The mind wonders, but, far from resisting the evidence, rejoices in the contemplation of the object. *Reason* (it is true) begins a search in order to explain the mystery by means of some more general agency already known; but if it fails to find it, it does not deny the fact which it cannot explain. But how can men of no common talents allow themselves so to be led away by the vulgar error of divines, as to make the submission of reason to the mysterious *facts* of experience a ground to demand a similar submission to *mysteries* which arise from certain *explanations* of language? Does the supposed mystery stand before us as a *fact*, as one of the mysteries of visible nature? By no means. Our whole theological *fact* is reduced to the presence of certain arbitrary marks, or characters, representing vocal sounds, which, in their turn, were used in a language now dead, to represent objects for the *most part* material and *universally* within man's knowledge, which are now supposed to express *figuratively* something spiritual, and quite beyond the knowledge and comprehension of man. Upon this *fact* alone the orthodox divines build their contradictory statements; and when they have raised their mighty structure of words which destroy each other's sense, they tell us that it is a *mystery;* and that, as we believe the mysteries of Nature, so must we surrender our understanding to the mysteries of their own creation. How can any man of sense be entangled in such a miserable fallacy? The existence of the pretended mysteries is the very question which divides the Christian world. Our observation cannot go beyond the words which some divines declare to assert the existence of the mystery. Renounce the *human exposition* from which the mystery arises, and it totally disappears. Does anything like this happen with the *mysteries of nature?* The mysteries of the Divine essence are not, cannot be, before our eyes; they are not, cannot be, even *verbally* in the Scriptures; for words are not able to express anything above the ideas of the human mind. What we find in the Scriptures are expressions couched in the *language of men;* consequently we must expect that they be *significant.* But divines contend that they *signify what men cannot understand.* They go further, and in *contradictory* language they tell you that they have laid before you what the Scripture contains; and when you answer that *contradictory language* is no language at all, they accuse you of *pride of Reason.* In a word, *they themselves* make the mysteries, and then want you to submit, as if those mysteries stood before you in the character of independent and unquestionable facts.

I cannot too earnestly beg your constant attention to the great difference between mysteries *to be explained* and mysteries *to be proved.* Reason submits to the former, because the existence of the mysterious fact is unquestionable; but when called upon to submit to the latter, because forsooth they also are *mysteries,* it turns away in disgust. The mysteries to which the reason of the Unitarian objects are not mysteries *proved*, are not even mysteries positively stated in divinely authorized language, but mysteries *conjectured* to lie concealed in that language: they are not unfrequently *verbal contradictions* which no rational language can be supposed to contain. If God, through his accredited messengers, had said, "The language in which I am to address you about myself is, when tried by the invariable laws of the mind, contradictory to itself, yet I command you to repeat it, and say that you believe the mysteries it envelops;"—if such a command could be *satisfactorily* proved, reason would have no right to refuse it; but when the Gospel is addressed to us in that same language by means of which we understand each other, we may well conceive that it was intended to be understood; when it is called a *Revelation*, we must expect to find it really a *disclosure;* something that will convey a clear sense to our minds; not downright contradictions—not *mysterious words*, which, like the ABRACADABRA of the Gnostics, is to save us from evil by the sound and shape of its letters.

The position of the orthodox Protestants who, having renounced only fragments of Popery, cherish its main root in their hearts, is to me exceedingly curious, though lamentable. What an awkward defence against Transubstantiation must a Trinitarian make who accuses the Unitarian of *pride of Reason* because he will not admit that the Athanasian Creed is *virtually* contained in the New Testament! I can imagine the cry of triumph which would be raised if a few manuscripts of high antiquity were to be discovered in some corner of the East containing the passage on the *three heavenly witnesses*. And yet such testimony could not be compared either in point of unanimity or positive assertion with the words, *This is my body—This is my blood.* I do not believe either *transubstantiation* or the *real presence;* but, wishing to be just and impartial, I must declare that the Protestant clamours against the *pride of Reason* place the opponents of those Catholic doctrines completely in the power of their adversaries. Let us imagine a short dialogue.

CATHOLIC.—Why do you not believe what Christ declares in the most positive and clear words?

PROTESTANT.—Because the expressions, taken in a literal sense, are absurd.

CATHOLIC.—Are they more absurd than the proposition, *Three is One, and One is Three?* a proposition which you (agreeing with us) consider as the very foundation of the "Catholic verity;" though nothing like those words is found in the genuine portions of the New Testament. Do you not consider, besides, that the word *absurd* does not properly apply to physical facts? That one substance be changed into another, implies no *absurdity;* but that *three* distinct persons, *each of whom is God, should be* ONE God, is certainly ABSURD TO US.

PROTESTANT.—Transubstantiation, certainly, does not sound so absurd as the statement of the Trinity; but then, on the other hand, we have the testimony of our senses against it.

CATHOLIC.—The senses, my friend, have nothing to do in the present case, for the *substantial qualities* of bread and wine remain working upon the senses: the substance alone is changed. Surely, you do not object to this kind of philosophy, for it is just that which saves us from contradictions in the statement of the Trinity.

PROTESTANT.—But can you suppose that Christ, addressing plain men, who never had dreamt of such philosophy, would so depend upon its influence as to expect that, without any further explanation, they would understand that the bread and wine had been changed into his own body and blood?

CATHOLIC.—Do you not, in the same manner, believe that, although there is no direct assertion, no words about Trinity in Unity, which can be compared to "*This is my body, This is my blood,*" Christ left it to be inferred from scattered passages, by the assistance of philosophical speculations about Nature, Substance, Persons *Mutual-in-being,** &c. &c. ?

PROTESTANT.—My reason submits in the one case and resists in the other.

CATHOLIC.—Are you not guilty of pride—the PRIDE OF REASON? Do you not reject the clearest declaration that language can be conceived to make, because it offends your PRIDE?

But I must conclude this Letter, and, with it, the subject. The whole system of theology contained in the Articles of the various Protestant Churches is purely a work of *Reason*, though, unfortunately, misemployed. Those Articles are *Logical Inferences;* and *Inferences* are, unquestionably, the work of Reason. Even the *theory* of the verbal inspiration of the writings from which such inferences are supposed to be drawn, could not, if granted, raise the *inferential work* above its human character, or warrant it against error. This being a proposition which no candid and intelligent man will deny, I will leave you to judge between those who doom to eternal perdition every one who denies the accuracy of those inferences, and those who, with my humble self, contend that eternal happiness cannot depend on the right choice of such *opinions*. Which of these two classes is justly charged with PRIDE OF REASON? If you still doubt, read, I request, any of the numerous works of *Orthodox* Divines, Churchmen and Dissenters, and settle with yourself to whom Dr. Johnson's definition does properly apply. Remember that the second signification

---

* I do not know a better way of translating that important word *Circumincessio*, or *going round into one another*, which is of so great importance in every *treatise on the Trinity.*

of PRIDE is, "insolence, rude treatment of others, insolent exultation." If, however, you have none of those works at hand, wait a short time; and the *Orthodox* reviews of these Letters will perfectly answer the purpose.*

* This prediction, as far as my knowledge of Reviews extends, has not yet been fulfilled. I have seen only one review of this work, in the British Critic, and a more friendly critique it is impossible to conceive. If this note should reach the author of that article, about whom I have not even a conjecture, I beg him to accept my most hearty thanks.

J. B. W.

Liverpool, March 30th, 1839.

APPENDICES AND NOTES.

APPENDIX I.

On the origin of the article before the word CHRIST.

(Postscript to Letter I., page 25.)

I HAVE in various passages added the article to the word Christ: the view from which this alteration arises had not fully opened itself before my mind when these Letters were published. The importance, however, of that view appears to me so great, that I propose to state it at full length, if my incessant sufferings should allow me to write a continuation to the present work. That I will earnestly strive to accomplish that task, I have no doubt. But in the mean time, I beg my readers to observe, that the practice of joining the words *Jesus* and *Christ*, as if they were one name, cannot be primitive. There can, indeed, exist little doubt that the original practice must have been that of writing *the* Christ, and Jesus *the* Christ. The great question between the disciples of Jesus of Nazareth and the Jews was, whether the title of Messiah should be given to that individual; whether *Jesus* was the *Messiah*, i.e. *the Christ*. Few, I believe, do not know that both *Christ* and *Messiah* mean the same thing, namely, the *Anointed*, i.e. the King.

Now, it is unquestionable that, about the time when Jesus presented himself in public, preaching the approach of THE KINGDOM, namely, the moral kingdom of the Messiah, the Christ, the Anointed, the notions which people attached to those words were extremely various. In conformity with these various notions of the Messiahship would the followers of Jesus form their notions of his dignity, knowledge, power, and other qualities. This, I conceive, was the primitive source of the *varieties* of Christians, which appear contemporaneously with the earliest propagation of the Gospel. All who before the birth of Jesus were joined in a kind of religious fellowship, of which the uniting principle was the expectation of a *moral*, not a *warlike* Christ, and had reduced their *internal* religion to an enlightened morality and a spiritual worship, would naturally profess themselves disciples of Jesus as soon as they heard of his preaching, and perceived its conformity with their own views. To me it appears very probable that the name *Christian* existed before Jesus, and that the reason why the *disciples* began to be called *Christians* at Antioch was, that many who already called themselves so, joined the disciples of the apostles. But I cannot at present develop the important consequences which I find to flow from this view; I only beg the candid reader to accustom himself to remember that *Christ* is a name of *office*, and consequently that the article must be understood before it, even where the text does not exhibit it. How is it possible that the early Christians should be guilty of such a solecism as that of using the words *Jesus Christ* as a name and surname, just as if, employing two perfect equivalents, we were to say *Joshua King?* Let the reader divest himself of that impression, and he will be prepared to distinguish between the man Jesus and the various attributes of his office—attributes which were conceived in a great variety of aspects, according to the previous notions which the primitive Jewish Christians had of the Christ or Messiah. Thus some light may be thrown upon the dark history of the early Christian theology; thus the phantom of a uniform Tradition of Doctrine will be finally chased away.

I cannot at present undertake the labour of examining Griesbach's various readings, in order to find how frequent are the traces of a second-hand addition of the word *Jesus* to the word *Christ;* but if it should be proved, as I am convinced it may, that *the Christ,* the *Messiah,* the *Logos,* are metaphorical expressions or verbal symbols of the only God in the manifestations of his supreme Reason, it will not be difficult to shew that many of the high-sounding passages usually applied to prove the Divinity of the man Jesus, were originally used in regard to the abstract Christ, the Messiah, *i.e.* of God himself, conceived as the Logos, or his supreme Reason, which is himself, as he manifests his nature in the creation and government of the world. To make this abstraction of the human mind a self-subsisting Person, is a monstrous materialization of a figure of language, which could not have entered the minds even of the Rabbins, among whom St. Paul learnt his Messianic phraseology. Still more absurd it is to crush into one the *imaginary* personality of the Christ of the Palestinian Jews (which is the same as the Logos of the Jews who lived in Egypt), and the personality of the man Jesus. I conclude by requesting such readers as have not studied the writings of the Alexandrian Jews, called the *Apocrypha*, those of Philo, and such works as disclose the doctrines prevalent in the Rabbinical schools, not' to take the hints I have thrown out as mere paradoxes.—*March* 20*th*, 1839.

After writing what precedes, I submitted to the labour of examining in a few books of the New Testament how many passages, where the Greek article is found before Χριστὸς, have been translated in the established Version without its English equivalent. The result of my examination is as follows:—

In Matthew, the article appears 11 times: in English only 3.
In Mark, ,, ,, 5 ,, ,, 2.
In Luke, ,, ,, 10 ,, ,, 3.
In John, ,, ,, 17 ,, ,, 9.
 and twice *that* instead of *the*.
In Acts, ,, ,, 14 ,, ,, not once;
 that is once used.
In Romans, ,, ,, 12 ,, ,, not once.

I have a strong suspicion that the English translators saw too frequently the Greek original through the Latin Version, with which they were familiar: the Latin language having no article, they were often led into the omission of it in English. What confirms me in this conjecture is the occasional use of *that*; for where the Latin translator thought it necessary to make *Christ* emphatical, he would use *ille* Christus, *illum* Christum. But this only by the way.—*March* 29*th*, 1839.

APPENDIX II.

A few Extracts from Professor Norton's Statement of Reasons for not believing the Doctrines of Trinitarians, &c. &c., *mentioned in the Preface of the present Work.**

Professor Norton, after mentioning that, in 1819, he had published a tract, to which he had given the title which is now prefixed to the work from which the following Extracts are taken, proceeds to say:—

" I have said, 'I resumed the task;' and the expression is appropriate; for the discussion is one in which no scholar or intellectual man can, at the present day, engage with alacrity. To the great body of enlightened individuals in all countries, to the generality of those who, on every subject but theology, are the guides of public opinion, it would be as incongruous to address an argument against the Trinity as an argument against Transubstantiation, or the imputation of Adam's sin, or the supremacy of the Pope, or the divine right of kings. These doctrines, once subjects of fierce contention, are all, in their view, equally obsolete. To disprove the

---

* The work of Professor Norton being still scarce in this country, I gladly avail myself of this opportunity of giving a few specimens, taken somewhat in connection with a few of the topics in the preceding little work, and of expressing my very high sense of the ability and learning displayed in that (according to my judgment) perfectly triumphant refutation of the established or orthodox doctrines on the Nature of God and the Person of Christ.

[I am very glad that this valuable work of Professor Norton is now known to a great number, among such as do not think it a Christian duty to close their eyes against everything that clashes with their established Orthodoxy.—*April 2nd*, 1839.]

Trinity will appear to many of whom I speak a labour as idle and unprofitable as the confutation of any other of those antiquated errors; and to engage in the task may seem to imply a theologian's ignorance of the opinions of the world, and the preposterous and untimely zeal of a recluse student, believing that the dogmas of his books still rule the minds of men. It would be difficult to find a recognition of the existence of this doctrine in any work of the present day of established reputation, not professedly theological. All mention of it is, by common consent, excluded from the departments of polite literature, moral science, and natural religion; and from discussions, written or oral, not purely sectarian, intended to affect men's belief or conduct. Should an allusion to it occur in any such production, it would be regarded as a trait of fanaticism, or as discovering a mere secular respect for some particular church. It is scarcely adverted to, except in works professedly theological; and theology, the noblest and most important branch of philosophy, has been brought into disrepute, so far, at least, as it treats of the doctrines of revealed religion, by a multitude of writers, who have seized upon this branch of it as their peculiar province, and who have been anything but philosophers.

"Why, then, argue against a doctrine which, among intelligent men, has fallen into neglect and disbelief? I answer, that the neglect and disbelief of this doctrine, and of other doctrines of like character, has extended to Christianity itself. It is from the public professions of nations calling themselves Christian, from the established creeds and liturgies of different churches or sects, and from the writings of those who have been reputed Orthodox in their day, that most men derive their notions of Christianity. But the treaties of European nations still begin with a solemn appeal to the 'Most Holy Trinity;' the doctrine is still the professed faith of every established church, and, as far as I know, of every sect which makes a creed its bond of communion: and if any one should recur to books, he would find it presented as an all-important distinction of Christianity by far the larger portion of divines. It is, in consequence, viewed by most men, more or less distinctly, as a part of Christianity. In connection with other doctrines, as false and more pernicious, it has been moulded into systems of religious belief, which have been publicly and solemnly substituted in the place of true religion. These systems have counteracted the whole evidence of divine revelation. The proof of the most important fact in the history of mankind, that the truths of religion have been left to be doubtfully and dimly discerned, but have been made known to us by God himself, has been overborne and rendered ineffectual by the nature of the doctrines ascribed to God. Hence it is that, in many parts of Europe, scarcely an intelligent and well-informed Christian is left. It has seemed as idle to inquire into the evidence of those systems which passed under the name of Christianity, as into the proof of the incarnations of Vishnu, or the divine mission of Mahomet. Nothing of the true character of our religion, nothing attesting its descent from heaven, was to be discovered amid the corruptions of the prevailing faith. On the contrary, they were so marked with falsehood and fraud, they so clearly discovered the baseness of their earthly origin, that, when imposed upon men as the peculiar doctrines of Christianity, those who regarded them as such were fairly relieved from the necessity of inquiring whether they had been taught by God. The internal evidence of Christianity was annihilated; and all other evidence is wasted when applied to prove that such doctrines have been revealed from heaven."—*Preface,* pp. i—vii.

———— "The doctrine (of the proper divinity of Christ) is proved to be false, because *it is evident from the Scriptures that none of those effects were produced which would necessarily have resulted from its first annunciation by Christ, and its subsequent communication by his Apostles.* The disciples of our Saviour must, at some period, have considered him merely as a man. Before he commenced his ministry, his relations and fellow-townsmen certainly regarded him as nothing more than a man. 'Is not this the carpenter, the son of Mary, the brother of James and Joseph, and of Judas and Simon? And are not his sisters here with us?'* At some particular period, the communication must have been made by our Saviour to his disciples, that he was not a mere man, but that he was, properly speaking and in the highest sense, God himself. The doctrines with which we are contending, and other doctrines of a similar character, have so obscured and confused the whole of Christianity, that

* Mark vi. 3.—"I have retained the words 'brothers' and 'sisters,' used in the common version, not thinking it important, in the connection in which the passage is quoted, to make any change in this rendering; but the relationship intended I believe to be that of cousins."

even its historical facts appear to be regarded by many scarcely in the light of real occurrences. But we *may* carry ourselves back in imagination to the time when Christ was on earth, and place ourselves in the situation of the first believers. Let us reflect for a moment on what would be the state of our feelings, if some one with whom we had associated as a man, were to declare to us that he was really God himself. If his character and works had been such as to command any attention to such an assertion, still through what an agony of incredulity, and doubt, and amazement, and consternation, must the mind pass, before it could settle down into a conviction of the truth of his declaration! And when convinced of its truth, with what unspeakable astonishment should we be overwhelmed! With what extreme awe, and entire prostration of every faculty, should we approach and contemplate such a being; if indeed man, in his present tenement of clay, could endure such intercourse with his Maker! With what a strong and unrelaxing grasp would the idea seize upon our minds! How continually would it be expressed in the most forcible language, whenever we had occasion to speak of him! What a deep and indelible colouring would it give to every thought and sentiment in the remotest degree connected with an agent so mysterious and so awful! But we perceive nothing of this state of mind in the disciples of our Saviour, but much that gives evidence of a very different state of mind. One may read over the first three Evangelists; and it must be by a more than ordinary exercise of ingenuity if he discover what may pass for an argument, that either the writers, or the numerous individuals of whom they speak, regarded our

Saviour as their Maker and God, or that he ever assumed that character..... Throughout the New Testament we find nothing which implies that such a most extraordinary change of feeling ever took place in the disciples of Christ, as must have been produced by the communication that their Master was God himself upon earth. Nowhere do we find the expression of those irresistible and absorbing sentiments which must have possessed their minds under the conviction of this fact. With this conviction, in what terms, for instance, would they have spoken of his crucifixion, and of the circumstances with which it was attended? The power of language would have sunk under them in the attempt to express their feelings: their words, when they approached the subject, would have been little more than a thrilling cry of horror and indignation. On this subject they did, indeed, feel most deeply; but can we think that St. Peter regarded his Master as God incarnate, when he thus addressed the Jews by whom Christ had just been crucified? 'Ye men of Israel, hear these words: Jesus of Nazareth, proved to you TO BE A MAN FROM GOD, by miracles, and wonders, and signs, which God did by him in the midst of you, as ye yourselves know, him, delivered up to you in conformity to the fixed will and foreknowledge of God, ye have crucified and slain by the hands of the heathen. Him has God raised to life.'— *Acts* ii. 22—24.

"But what has been stated are not the only consequences which must have followed from the communication of the doctrine in question. It cannot be denied by those who hold the doctrine of the Deity of Christ, that, however satisfactorily it may be explained, and however well it may be reconciled with that fundamental principle of religion to which the Jews were so strongly attached—the doctrine of the Unity of God—yet it does, or may, at first sight, appear somewhat inconsistent with it. From the time of the Jew who is represented by Justin Martyr as disputing with him, about the middle of the second century, to the present period, it has always been regarded by the unbelieving Jews with abhorrence. They have considered the Christians as no better than idolaters; as denying the first truth of religion. But the unbelieving Jews, in the time of the Apostles, opposed Christianity with the utmost bitterness and passion; they sought on every side for objections to it. There was much in its character to which the believing Jews could hardly be reconciled. The Epistles are full of statements, explanations, and controversy, relating to questions having their origin in Jewish prejudices and passions. With regard, however, to this doctrine, which, if it had been taught, the believing Jews must have received with the utmost difficulty, and to which the unbelieving Jews would have manifested the most determined opposition—with regard to this doctrine, there is no trace of any controversy. But if it had ever been taught, it must have been the main point of attack and defence between those who assailed and those who supported Christianity. There is nothing ever said in its explanation; but it must have required, far more than any other doctrine, to be explained, illustrated, and enforced; for it appears not only irreconcilable with the Unity of God, but equally so with that of the humanity of our Saviour; and yet both these doctrines, it seems, were to be maintained in connection with it.

It must have been necessary, therefore, to state it as clearly as possible, to exhibit it in its relations, and carefully to guard against the misapprehensions to which it is so liable on every side. Especially must care have been taken to prevent the gross mistakes into which the Gentile converts from polytheism were likely to fall. Yet, so far from any such clearness of statement and fulness of explanation, the whole language of the New Testament in relation to this subject, is (as I have before said) a series of enigmas, upon the supposition of its truth. The doctrine, then, is never defended in the New Testament, though unquestionably it would have been the main object of attack, and the main difficulty in the Christian system. It is never explained, though no doctrine could have been so much in need of explanation. On the contrary, upon the supposition of its truth, the Apostles express themselves in such a manner, that, if it had been their purpose to darken and perplex the subject, they could not have done it more effectually. And, still more, this doctrine is never insisted upon as a necessary article of faith; though it is now represented by its defenders as lying at the foundation of Christianity. With a few exceptions, the passages in which it is imagined to be taught are introduced incidentally, the attention of the writer being principally directed to some other topic, and can be regarded only as accidental notices of it. It appears, then, that while other questions of far less difficulty (for instance, the circumcision of the Gentile converts) were subjects of such doubts and controversy that even the authority of the Apostles was barely sufficient to establish the truth, this doctrine, so extraordinary, so obnoxious, and so hard to be under-

stood, was introduced in silence, and received without hesitation, dislike, opposition, or misapprehension. There are not many propositions to be proved or disproved merely by moral evidence which are more incredible."*
Ib. pp. 37—40.

On the Interpretation of Language.

"Supposing the doctrines maintained by Trinitarians to be capable of proof, the state of the case between them and their opponents would be this: They quote certain texts, and explain them in a sense which, as they believe, supports their opinions. We maintain that the words were intended to express a very different meaning. How is the question to be decided? We do not deny that there are certain expressions in these texts which, nakedly considered, *will bear* a Trinitarian sense; how is it then to be ascertained whether this sense or some other was intended by the writer?

"In order to answer this question, it is necessary to enter into some explanation concerning the nature of language and the principles of interpretation. The art of interpretation derives its origin from the *intrinsic ambiguity of language.* What I mean to express by this term is the fact, that a very large portion of sentences, *considered in themselves*, that is, *if regard be had merely to the words of which they are composed*, are capable of expressing not one meaning only, but two or more different meanings; or (to state this fact in other terms)

---

* This consideration, since it presented itself to me, long before I saw it thus luminously developed by Professor Norton, carried full conviction to my mind.—J. B. W.

that in very many cases, the same sentence, like the same single word, may be used to express various and often very different senses. Now in a great part of what we find written concerning the interpretation of language, and in a large portion of the specimens of criticism which we meet with, especially upon the Scriptures, this fundamental truth, this fact which lies at the very bottom of the art of interpretation, has either been overlooked, or not regarded in its relations and consequences. It may be illustrated by a single example. St. John thus addresses the Christians to whom he was writing, in his first Epistle, ii. 20—'*Ye have an anointing from the Holy One, and know all things.*'

"If we consider these words in themselves merely, we shall perceive how uncertain is their signification, and how many different meanings they may be used to express. The first clause, 'Ye have an anointing from the Holy One,' may signify,

"1. *Through the favour of God, ye have become Christians or believers in Christ;* anointing being a ceremony of consecration, and Christians being considered as consecrated and set apart from the rest of mankind.

"2. Or it may mean, *Ye have been truly sanctified in heart and life;* a figure borrowed from outward consecration being used to denote inward holiness.

"3. Or, *Ye have been endued with miraculous powers;* consecrated as prophets and teachers in the Christian community.

"4. Or, *Ye have been well instructed in the truths of Christianity.* (See *Wetstein's Notes* on this passage, and on 1st Tim. iv. 7.)

"I forbear to mention other meanings which the word

anointing might be used to express. These are sufficient for our purpose.

"The term *Holy One*, in such a relation as it holds to the other words in the present sentence, may denote either God, or Christ, or some other being.

"*Ye know all things*, literally expresses the meaning, *ye have the attribute of omniscience*. Beside this meaning, it may signify, *ye are fully acquainted with all the objects of human knowledge;* or, *ye know every truth connected with Christianity;* or, *ye have all the knowledge necessary to form your faith and direct your conduct;* or the proposition may require some other limitation; for *all things* is one of those terms the meaning of which is continually to be restrained and modified by a regard to the subject present to the mind of the writer.

"This statement may afford some imperfect notion of the various senses which the words before us may be used to express, and of the uncertainty that must exist about their meaning when they are regarded without reference to those considerations by which it ought to be determined. I say, imperfect, because we have really kept one very important consideration in mind, that they were written by an Apostle to a Christian community. Putting this out of view, it would not be easy to fix the limit of their possible meanings. It must be remembered that this passage has been adduced merely by way of illustration; and that, if it were necessary, an indefinite number of similar examples might be quoted."—*Ib.* pp. 90—92.

It is absolutely necessary to stop in this selection, by doing violence to the feeling of delight and admiration which invites the selector to proceed, as he turns page after page. Let no sincere Christian deceive himself into a persuasion that he has done justice to the question between the Unitarians and the Orthodox till he has impartially studied Professor Norton's REASONS. This praise, however, is not meant to be exclusive: on the contrary, I am of opinion that in many cases it would be difficult to decide whether that work, or Mr. Yates's VINDICATION, mentioned in my Preface, would be preferable.

APPENDIX III.

Passages of Scripture which have been alleged to prove the former Existence of an Apostolical Creed, explained.

MANY of my readers will require no apology for a rather long quotation from the CONFESSIONAL of Archdeacon Blackburne; a book which is now seldom in the hands of theological students, though the ability and learning it displays against the abuse of ecclesiastical power will at all times deserve the praise of every lover of *spiritual* freedom. I shall take also the liberty of inserting the paragraph which leads to the subject of this Appendix.

"I cannot leave this view of the connection between these two prelates, *Tillotson* and *Burnet*, without a short reflection on these *trimming* methods in matters of religion. When were they ever known to succeed? And where were they ever known to conciliate the mind of any one of those unreasonable zealots to whose humour they were accommodated? We of this generation* have lived to see how greatly Archbishop *Tillotson* was mistaken, in thinking to win over the high churchmen of those days by his healing expedients. His gentle, lenitive spirit was to their bigotry what oil is to the fire. Bishop Burnet's friendship for the Archbishop carried him into these measures, contrary to his natural bent, and in mere complaisance to the Archbishop's apprehensions of a storm, which he dreaded above all other things. And I remember to have heard some old men rejoice, that *Burnet* was kept down by *Tillotson's* influence from pushing the reformation of the Church to an extremity that might have endangered the Government itself. Some of these men, however, might have remembered, that when the Archbishop was no longer at hand to temper *Burnet's* impetuosity, the latter had prudence sufficient to balance his courage, and to keep him from attempting what he had sense enough to perceive was impracticable. But, after all, what has been the consequence of *Tillotson's* gentleness and *Burnet's* complaisance for the times? Even this; these two eminent lights of the English Church could not have been more opposed while they lived, or more abused and vilified since they died, had they firmly and vigorously promoted, at all adventures, the reformation in the Church of *England*, which they were both of them deeply conscious she

* I believe the edition of the *Confessional* I am using (1766) is the earliest.

very much wanted. But, after all, if what Bishop *Burnet* has offered under all these disadvantages will not justify the Church of *England* in requiring subscription to the Thirty-nine Articles, we may venture to conclude, without any just imputation of temerity, that this service will hardly be more effectually performed by men of another stamp, who may probably engage in it with more alacrity and less circumspection. What the good Bishop has said on this behalf (on subscription) we now propose to consider.

"His Lordship begins with stating the seeming impropriety 'of making such a collection of tenets the standard of the doctrine of a Church that (according to his Lordship) is deservedly valued by reason of her moderation. This (says the Bishop) seems to be a departing from the simplicity of the first ages, which yet we set up for a pattern.'*

"This objected impropriety (which, by the way, his Lordship exceedingly strengthens and illustrates by an induction of particulars) he rather endeavours to palliate and excuse, or, as he terms it, *explain*, than to deny or confute. He gives us an historical recital of the practice of former times, to shew that our Church acts after a precedent of long standing. To this no other answer is necessary than that this was the practice of times which were not remarkable either for their *moderation* or *simplicity*, and of whose example the Church of *England* cannot avail herself, consistently with her pretensions to these two amiable qualities.†

* Introduction, p. 1.

† To illustrate this truth, *Dr. Mosheim's Compendious View of Ecclesiastical History* may be consulted, from the time of *Constantine* down-

" But it seems this practice was originally the practice of the Apostles; a consideration which will not only authorize our imitation, but strongly imply the utility and edification of the thing itself.

"'There was a form (says his Lordship) settled very early in most churches. This St. Paul, in one place, calls *The form of doctrine that was delivered;* in another place, *The form of sound words*, which those who were fixed by the Apostles in particular churches had received from them. These words of his do import a *standard* or *fixed formulary*, by which all doctrines were to be examined.'*

"The passages here referred to are Rom. vi. 17; 1st Tim. iv. 6, to which are added, in the margin, 1st Tim. vi. 3; 2nd Tim. i. 13; and the Greek words in these several passages, which are supposed to signify this *standard* or *fixed formulary*, run thus:—τύπον διδαχῆς —ὑποτύπωσιν ὑγιαινόντων λόγων—τοῖς λόγοις τῆς πίστεως, καὶ τῆς καλῆς διδασκαλίας—ὑγιαίνουσι λόγοις τοῖς τοῦ Κυρίου ἡμῶν Ἰησοῦ Χριστοῦ καὶ τῇ κατ' εὐσέβειαν διδασκαλίᾳ.

"Now, when a capable and unprejudiced reader considers the variety of expression in these several passages, he will probably be inclined to think that a *fixed formulary* of doctrine is the last thing a plain man would look for in them. A *fixed formulary*, one would think, should have a *fixed title*. Nor is it at all probable that one and the same form of words should be described in terms which may denote a hundred different forms.

"To enter into a just criticism on these expressions

wards; and with greater advantage, in *Dr. Maclaine's* English translation lately published.—*Note in the* " *Confessional.*"

* Introduction, p. 2.

would be tedious and unnecessary. Suffice it to observe, after very competent judges, that τύπος διδαχῆς and ὑποτύπωσις ὑγιαινόντων λόγων appear to refer rather to the *exemplification* of the Christian doctrine in the *practice* of pious believers than to any *form of words*. The *doctrine* is *one* thing, and the *type* of the doctrine *another*. The doctrine is and must be expressed by, and consequently contained in, *some* form of words. But the *type* of that *form* must be something different from the form itself: and the general acceptation of the word τύπος points out the *practical exemplification* of the doctrine to be the thing here intended. The text, Rom. vi. 17, is, it must be owned, obscure and difficult; but without giving this sense to the words τύπος διδαχῆς, it is absolutely unintelligible.* And whatever is the signification of τύπος here, must be the meaning of ὑποτύπωσις, 2nd Tim. i. 13.†

"Again, the literal English of ὑγιαίνοντες λόγοι, is *healing* or *salutary words;* that is, the words of salvation or

---

* "See *Grotius* and *Bengelius's* Gnomon upon the place. Τυπος. Typus, vestigium, figura, exemplar, forma. *Hen. Stephens.* Acts xxiii. 25, τυπος is the *literal copy* of *Lysias's* epistle to *Felix*, not the sum or abridgment of it."—*Note in the "Confessional."*

† "The word is but once more to be found in the New Testament, viz. 1st Tim. i. 16 ; where the Apostle says *he found* mercy—πρὸς ὑποτύπωσιν τῶν μελλόντων πιστεύειν, &c., for *a pattern;* which is the same thing as an *example* of the doctrine of pardon and mercy through Christ. In what sense the word τύπος was afterwards used, may be seen in Mills's translation of *Bruys's* History of the Popes, Vol. I. p. 428 ; where an instrument or edict of the Emperor *Constans* for the pacification of the disputes concerning the two wills of Christ, is called the *type;* which instrument contained no formulary of doctrine, but only enjoined that the parties at variance should abide by the Scriptures, the five œcumenical councils, and the plain and simple passages of the fathers."—*Note in the "Confessional."*

eternal life. Our translators have rendered the Greek particle by the equivocal words *sound* and *wholesome*, which signified, I suppose, in their ideas, the same as *orthodox*.

"If you ask where these *healing words* are to be found; I answer, in the Scriptures; sometimes, perhaps, abridged and comprehended in some short summaries which occur in Paul's Epistles to *Timothy* and *Titus*. But these are evidently not the *fixed formularies* his Lordship means, as the certain consequence of that must have been, that no man or body of men whatsoever could have had the least authority to add to them, or enlarge them in any future time.

"And if any other *standard* or *formulary* is meant, it then comes to our turn to ask the question, Where is it to be found? What is become of it? For that it should be lost, or drop into utter oblivion, if it once had a real existence, is wholly incredible.

"In answer to this demand, the Bishop gives us to understand, 'that by a *fixed formulary* he does not mean *one precise* and invariable form of words, which he thinks improbable the Apostles should leave behind them. For his Lordship observes, that the first apologists for Christianity, when they deliver a short abstract of the Christian faith, do all vary from one another, both as to the order and as to the words themselves: whence he thinks it more probable that they received these short abstracts from the Apostles themselves with some variation.

"But, surely, the moment you admit of *variations*, not only the *idea* of a *fixed formulary*, but even the *use* of *any* formulary, as a *standard* or *test* of *all* doctrines, immediately vanishes away. There must be left in such *varying* formularies room for doubtful and precarious judgments; and the Scriptures alone, in such cases, must be the *dernier ressort.* And if so, why might they not as well have been admitted to decide in the first instance?"—*The Confessional,* p. 66, et seq. The sequel of this passage, indeed the whole work, should be particularly noticed in the present times.

APPENDIX IV.

On the Old Testament as a supposed Standard of Orthodoxy.

THE frequently quoted words of Paul (2nd Tim. iii. 16, 17) will probably occur to many, as clearly opposing my statement. Let us consider those words, divesting ourselves of *established* prejudices. "All Scripture is given by inspiration of God, and is profitable for doctrine, for reproof, for correction, for instruction in righteousness; that the man of God may be perfect, thoroughly furnished unto all good works."

I have a few observations to lay before the dispassionate reader.

The Greek word θεόπνευστος is not only figurative, but may *possibly* represent two *figures,* which are the reverse of each other; something *breathed out by God,* and something *breathing out God.* It is true that the Lexicons, so far as I have been able to consult them, limit the word in question to the first signification. I am aware also that the best grammarians exclude from the class of compounds which are capable both of the active and the passive signification, as (μητροκτονος, θεοτοκος, marking the change by the accent) those which end in τος, probably because they are derived not from the middle but the *passive* preterit. But since such derivatives from the passive, as ἄπνευστος, εὔπνευστος, mean, *he that breathes not, he that breathes well*, the supposition that θεόπνευστος may signify *Deum spirans*, or, as it might be expressed in English, *breathing of God*, may be not well grounded but it cannot be absurd. After all, it seems strange that the fact of *inspiration* should depend so much on a delicate point of grammatical criticism.

In the next place, I request a serious attention to St. Paul's enumeration of the purposes for which he considers the Hebrew Scriptures as eminently useful. The impartial reader should, in his mind, compare, as he proceeds, the various parts of this enumeration with the pretended destination of those writings, to settle the disputes of *scientific* theology, and thus to fix *Orthodoxy*.

1. Those Scriptures, according to Paul, had the power to make Timothy (a Jew) *wise unto salvation through that faith which is in Christ Jesus*. That the Hebrew Scriptures were so ordained by Providence as to lead the upright, candid, and virtuous Jews to Christ, cannot be denied. 2. Those Scriptures are profitable for teaching (διδασκαλίαν). The Jews had, indeed, no other *national* means of instruction. 3. The Hebrew Scriptures are profitable for reproof (ἔλεγχον); and unquestionably, to

a Jew, as long as the polity existed in compliance with which Paul had circumcised Timothy (not for any value which Paul himself set on circumcision, but "because of the Jews"*), the Hebrew Scriptures were the standard by which the conduct of every member of the nation, who had not arrived at the full conscientious conviction of the abolition of the law through Christ, should be judged. 4. The Hebrew Scriptures are profitable for *correction* (ἐπανόρθωσιν), *i.e. setting right again*. This is a declaration almost identical with that immediately preceding. 5. The Hebrew Scriptures are profitable for instruction (παιδείαν, *i.e. elementary* instruction (in righteousness (δικαιοσύνῃ), *i.e.* the correct conduct of a Jew; who, if he was observant of the law, was, in the language of the New Testament, called δίκαιος.

This more rhetorical than logical enumeration concludes with a sentence which, in general terms, expresses the *final end* of the advantages offered by the Hebrew Scriptures to a pious Jew; namely, "*that the man of God*"† (*i.e.* a man whose life, like that of the ancient prophets, is devoted to the object of spreading the principles and sentiments of piety) *may be* COMPETENT (ἄρτιος), *thoroughly furnished (fitted out—*ἐξηρτισμένος) for every good work (*i.e.* every duty of his office).

When the utmost shall have been done to increase the significancy of every phrase in this passage, I wish the reader impartially to judge whether St. Paul's *occasional* praise of the Hebrew Scriptures, and his list of the

* Acts xvi. 3.
† Compare 1st Samuel ix. 6; 1st Kings xiii. 6; 2nd Kings i. 9.

APPENDIX. 157

advantages which may be derived from them (especially by Jews, before the total abolition of their politico-religious constitution), can in a satisfactory manner prove that the Apostle was thinking of an *inspired verbal rule of faith*, by which *scientific* disputes in theology—much less in physics, chronology, &c.—should be settled, as by the intervention of an oracle. Observe, however, how the Old Testament is used among us. Suppose a divine denies that the *literal* sense gives the true meaning of the beginning of Genesis; we instantly hear an indignant cry against the impiety of such a view. But why? Has St. Paul given us any rule to ascertain *to which of the senses* of every passage in Scripture it is that the word θεόπνευστος applies? And since he has not, should we not take that omission as a proof that the word which the established version translates "inspiration of God," means only a *general* derivation from God, which leaves the Christian at liberty to expound *individual* passages so as to prevent their opposing the *originally divine light of our* REASON, fully assisted by the SPIRIT of the Gospel? By what clear title does any man accuse another of impiety when that man uses his intellectual liberty?

Were there a judge of the sense of Scripture divinely appointed; were that appointment so made as to allow of no reasonable doubt; to act against the decisions of that judge would deserve the condemnation to which clear offences against divine authority are liable. But since we have been left to judge of the sense of the Scriptures *for ourselves*, every man, after exerting his means and faculties to the best of his power, must adhere to what he understands. He must, of course, think others *wrong;* but, as he should remember his own liability to error, he ought to abstain from condemning them as guilty of sin and impiety. To act as most divines act at present, is a most unchristian presumption.

NOTES.

NOTE TO PAGE 15.

On 2nd John 7—11.

The passages of Scripture which seem to give an appearance of probability to the essentially intolerant notion that Orthodoxy is necessary to salvation, or which (to speak more properly) disturb the conviction which Reason, enlightened by the Scriptures, is apt to produce against that notion in candid, unsuperstitious minds, are very few. This, by itself, is a strong proof to me that the intolerant interpretation commonly given to them cannot be true; for Providence would not have committed so important and practical a declaration to a few incidental expressions. In the Trinitarian question, especially, this consideration is to me more powerful than any direct interpretation of individual passages. But, in regard to our present subject, I think it necessary to draw the attention of the reader to that passage of the 2nd Epistle of John, which I have constantly found to be the last refuge of intolerance defeated by argument. But although I have carried on my argument without questioning either the full inspiration (as it is called) of the Scriptures, or the authenticity of commonly received passages, it would be doing wrong to the cause of spiritual freedom if I did not mention in this place the fact, that the Second and the Third Epistles which bear the name of John, were among those writings of which the genuineness was disputed in the early ages of the Church. Eusebius, whose authority may be said to be the chief foundation of our present canon, classes those Epistles with writings which at a later period were totally excluded from the catalogue of *Holy Scriptures*, such as the Acts of Paul, the Shepherd, the Revelation of Peter and the Epistle of Barnabas. This being premised, that the intelligent and candid reader may not be without that degree of light which may be derived from this fact, I will proceed to the examination of the above-mentioned passage. But to save inquirers the trouble of seeking for the passage in the New Testament, I shall copy it here. I will also give in italics the expressions which appear to me to deserve particular attention.

Verse 6. "And this is love, that we walk after his commandments. This is the *commandment* (namely, that we love one another—see v. 5 and John xiv. 15—21) that, as ye have heard from the beginning, ye should walk in it. (V. 7): For many deceivers are entered into the world, who confess not that Jesus Christ is come in the flesh. This is a deceiver and an antichrist. (V. 8): Look to yourselves, that we lose not those things which we have wrought, but that we receive a full reward. (V. 9): Whosoever transgresseth, and *abideth not in the doctrine of* (the) *Christ, hath not God. He that abideth in the doctrine of* (the) *Christ, he hath both the Father and the Son.* (V. 10): *If there come any unto you, and bring not this doctrine, receive him not into your house, neither bid him God-speed:* (v. 11), for he that biddeth him God-speed, is partaker of his evil deeds."

I wish the reader to consider the great probability (to me, certainty) that the writer means the same thing by *commandment*, ἐντολή, as by διδαχή, *doctrine*. To be convinced of this, nothing more is necessary than to refer to v. 9, and compare it with v. 10, c. xv. and v. 23, c. xiv. of the Gospel of John. The reward of keeping Christ's words, commandments, or doctrine (for the context shews that they are various names given to the same thing—*i. e.* charity, love to God, and to one another), is the coming of the *Father and the Son* to him, and making their abode with him. The very same result is in the Epistle attributed, in less figurative words, to the keeping the *doctrine* of Christ. *He that abideth in the doctrine of Christ, he hath both the Father and the Son;* or is in full possession of Christianity, which consists not only in the acknowledgment of God, but in the acceptance of Christ as a guide to Him. From this comparison of passages, by keeping in mind the *practical* character which John gives to Christianity, and by remembering that he reduces it to love to God, as known through Christ, and to our brethren, for the sake of the love which Christ deserves from us, we may be convinced that nothing was farther from the Evangelist's thoughts than the condemnation of *theoretical* doctrines. What he condemns is the *denial* of the existence of Christ, and the consequent denial of his *doctrine,* his *great commandment,* his *peculiar doctrine of love to God and man;* that love which necessarily produces moral obedience.

And here I must observe the unjustifiable rendering of v. 7, "deceivers ... who confess not that Jesus Christ IS COME in the flesh." The Greek participle present, $\dot{\epsilon}\rho\chi\delta\mu\epsilon\nu o\nu$ (Lat. *venientem*), has evidently the force of an adjective in this place. The difference is most important. The translation should be, *not confessing* (or not acknowledging) *him who is come in the flesh, Jesus Christ*—literally, Jesus Christ, the *coming* in the flesh. Thus everything is plain and consistent. John is not concerned with metaphysical and mystic doctrines. Such as deny the *existence of the man Christ,* whose love to mankind is the great acting spring of the new *doctrine* ($\delta\iota\delta\alpha\chi\dot{\eta}$); those who, probably in consequence of that theory which induced others to say that the *resurrection was past,* denied that the Christ had existed, and made the whole of Christianity a *figurative, moral fable;* such men were true *Antichrists,* destroyers of Christianity, and should be carefully avoided by the Christian congregations, when, as preachers, as men who carried about the *doctrine* (see v. 10), they claimed those rights of *maintenance* and *encouragement** which (as we find in St. Paul's Epistles) were considered to be the right of the true apostles and messengers of the Gospel.†

Note to page 34.

On the word Salvation.

No reflecting reader of the New Testament can but have observed the indistinct and vague meaning of the word *salvation*. Those who are blindly guided by the impressions left upon their infant minds by the undisputed authority of catechisms and nurses, imagine that no doubt can arise upon the meaning of salvation, condemnation, and the other words grammatically connected with them: *Salvation* must mean going to heaven; Damnation, being doomed to eternal fire. But these are arbitrary notions. The Greek word which is translated *salvation*, as well as the expression, *to be saved*, was part of the established language of the chief Pagan schools of moral philosophy. From the language of the moral writers it was borrowed for the writings of the New Testament; and as the authors of those writings have nowhere explained such expressions, but taken it for granted that their readers would understand them, we have a sufficient ground to infer that they used them in the common and established sense of *moral safety* on the one side, and *moral reprehensibleness* on the other. The passages of Greek writers which prove this statement would occupy too much space: they are well known to all good scholars who allow themselves mental freedom. The bare statement of the fact

---

* Observe attentively what is forbidden in v. 11, viz. *lodging and entertainment*.

† See 2nd Tim. ii. 18; 1st Thess. ii. 6.

above alluded to, is enough for my present purpose, which is to put the plain but intelligent reader upon his guard against interpretations of the original language of Scripture which have no ground for their popularity but the despotic sway of the various clerical bodies, called churches, over the helpless minds of children born under their domination.

The following passage of Plutarch, in the Life of Æmilius Paulus, which drew my attention some years ago as I was reading those interesting lives, with no view whatever to theological controversy, may be of some interest to scholars—

Ταῦτα μὲν οὖν ἡ ἱστορία λογίζεσθαι καὶ παρεπισκοπεῖν δίδωσι τοῖς ΣΩ'ΖΕΣΘΑΙ ΒΟΥΛΟΜΕ'ΝΟΙΣ. *Plut. Paul. Æmil.* v. "So much instruction does history suggest to the consideration of those who are willing to profit by it."—*Langhorne's Translation.*

Is there among the D.D.'s that can construe a Greek passage, any one who, if in the above sentence the words ἡ ἱστορία had been changed into ἡ .ταραβολὴ, and the whole attributed to Saint Chrysostom, would not have translated it: "So much instruction does this parable suggest to the consideration of those who wish to be saved"?—(*March* 22, 1839.)

On opening a Greek Testament, which I had not used for some time, I have found, in reference to Acts ii. 47, the two following verses of Theognis, in my own hand—

ἀλλὰ δόλους τ', ἀπάτας τε, πολυπλοκίας τ' ἐφίλησαν
οὕτως, ὡς ἄνδρες μηκέτι σωζόμενοι.

Paraineseis, vv. 67, 68.

NOTE TO PAGE 93.

On the Spiritual Assistance promised by CHRIST.

WHATEVER may be the means by which the assistance which, under the name Holy Spirit, is promised to sincere Christians, is communicated, the effect must appear in the character of *reasonable motives* operating upon the will. The *mystical* signification which the term *spiritual* has had for ages among most Christians, cannot be proved to have been intended by the writers of the New Testament, who evidently used it in the sense of *mental* or *intellectual.* Much less is there any ground for supposing the assistance in question to be miraculous. The established laws of our intellectual and moral nature, and the nature of the Christian principle, seem quite sufficient for the fulfilment of the promise of Christ. "Every one that asketh receiveth; and he that seeketh findeth; and to him that knocketh it shall be opened,"—are (as we may infer from the manner of the assertion) established laws of the moral world; yet they mean the same thing as the promise of assistance. The whole view of the subject is beautifully brought to one point in the affecting words of Jesus, as recorded in Luke xi. 13 : "If ye then, being evil, know how to give good gifts unto your children, how much more shall your heavenly Father give the Holy Spirit to them that ask him!" An assistance which so regularly and *naturally* flows from the character of our heavenly Father, cannot be supposed to be bestowed by occasional and extraordinary exertions of divine power. It must take place as an established law, whenever the free moral agent, man, shall fulfil the conditions required.

NOTE TO A PASSAGE FROM FENELON, PAGE 108.

THERE is not a true scholar who will not thank me for shewing a remarkable coincidence between the words of the most amiable of Bishops, and those of the most amiable of Sovereigns, the Emperor Marcus Aurelius Antoninus. I think it probable that Fenelon must have habitually studied that treasure of wisdom, the *Memorandums* of Marcus Aurelius, commonly called his *Meditations;* for it is impossible that a lover of virtue can become well acquainted with that book, and not make it his daily companion.

Lib. viii. § 54. Μηκέτι μόνον συμπνεῖν τῷ περιέχοντι ἀέρι, ἀλλὰ ἤδη καὶ συμφρονεῖν τῷ περιέχοντι πάντα νοερῷ· οὐ γὰρ ἧττον ἡ νοερὰ δύναμις πάντῃ κέχυται καὶ διαπεφοίτηκε τῷ σπάσαι δυναμένῳ, ἤπερ ἡ ἀερώδης τῷ ἀναπνεῦσαι δυναμένῳ.

(Remember) "not only to breathe with the surrounding air, but also to be wise with the intelligence which enfolds all things; for the intelligent power is not less universally diffused, or less spread about, than the aerial, for him that is able to draw it."

The simile of the Light is also found, Lib. ix. § 8.

ADDITIONAL APPENDIX.

PORTION OF A LETTER TO REV. JAMES MARTINEAU FROM REV. J. BLANCO WHITE.*

June, 1836.

"My dear Friend,—The constant and almost involuntary employment of my mind on the painful subject of the divisions of Christians, produces an habitual desire to exert myself in the as yet hopeless work of diminishing the sources of that great evil.

* * * * * *

"There is a point from which all writers on Christian liberty seem instinctively to recoil: it is, the *authority* of the Bible. And yet whilst that authority remains undefined,—as long as all Christians are taught to look upon the whole collection, from Genesis to the end of the book of Revelation, as the immediate and direct *Word of God*, and oracle before which human judgment is bound to submit, renouncing its natural rights,—to talk of *spiritual* liberty, under such a mental yoke, is almost mockery. I have already stated, in my 'Observations on Heresy and Orthodoxy,' some of the results of a long and anxious examination of this subject. I have proved, as I conceive, that it would be more consistent with intellectual or spiritual freedom to live under the whole

---

* Reprinted from the Appendix to "The Rationale of Religious Inquiry," Fourth Edition, by permission of Dr. Martineau.

Mosaic routine of *external* practices, than under the obligation of receiving the philosophy, history, chronology, and astronomy of the Bible. Whoever does not feel this, cannot be a judge of this question. Mental freedom,— the right to give free scope to the noblest powers of his nature,—would be a dead letter to such a man.

* * * * * *

"(9.) But I must condense what I have to say, and for that purpose I beg to call your attention to the fact, that the obscure and indefinite notions of such a *moral* duty in regard to the Bible cannot be traced to any legitimate source. This absence of an unquestionable and clear divine injunction is sufficient to upset the whole theory which supposes Christianity to have its ground in the Bible. I beg to be clearly understood upon this subject. In denying that the *authority* of the Scriptures is the foundation of Christianity, I am far from asserting that the Bible is useless to Christians. 'The question is not' (I will say with Barclay, the apologist of the Quakers, whose work contains admirable hints on this subject), 'The question is not what may be profitable or helpful, but what is absolutely necessary. Many things may contribute to further a work, which yet are not the main thing that makes the work go on.'* What I oppose is, the almost universal notion, that the first and essential condition of being a Christian is, to submit to the *authority* of the Scriptures. This is a gratuitous assumption. To demand *respect* for the various books of the Bible, in proportion to the *critical* probability that they are the writings of apostles or prophets, is rational; but respect is not submission, nor does

* Apology for the Quakers, Prop. II. § iv.

respect exclude examination and dissent. The exclusion of these inalienable rights of a free, rational creature, must be grounded upon direct, unquestionable, and definite divine command; and such command has never been made known to men. Conjecture and inference are of no avail. My right to judge is clearer than any *conjecture* that God wishes me to renounce it.

"(10.) I have indeed been persuaded, for many, many years (though the importance of the subject has made me try and (as it were) ripen my persuasion by keeping it in my bosom), that the theory which makes Christianity rest upon the infallibility of the Bible is much more groundless than that which places it on the infallibility of the successor of St. Peter and his Church. Both these theories want truth; but the latter (the Roman Catholic theory) is consistent within itself, and derives a very great plausibility from its perfect efficiency in settling questions among those that embrace it as emanated from the authority of Christ. The semi-Protestant view, which, admitting the necessity of a right faith (meaning assent to certain metaphysical and historical assertions), appeals in ultimate judgment to certain writings, must at once betray its groundlessness to every one who will dispassionately consider the total insufficiency of the proposed means for the attainment of the desired end. Grant the most literal and minute inspiration to the whole Bible, and it will still be found totally inadequate to the purpose of settling questions as to its own meaning, when such questions arise.

"(11.) It might indeed be supposed that the experience of three centuries would have opened the eyes of all Protestants on this point, and that they would now

ADDITIONAL APPENDIX.   169

begin to perceive that Luther fell into an egregious error when he imagined that a system of orthodoxy, in the same spirit as that of the Church of Rome, could be maintained upon the basis of the *written* authority of the Scriptures; that the idea of a *saving orthodoxy* could have even the slightest colouring of truth without a living rule of faith. But the clearest demonstrations on these subjects lose their power when superstitious fear paralyzes the logical faculty. Protestants of all denominations continue to denounce perdition on those who disagree with them on what they themselves have decreed to be *essentials;* and, in spite of their long experience of the insufficiency of the Bible to put an end to these disgraceful feuds, they go on crying and protesting that it is the fault of their opponents,—that if those unfortunate men would only see certain texts in a certain light (*i.e.* the light of the divines who think themselves aggrieved by the opponents' obstinacy), the Protestants might soon rival the Church of Rome in unity.

"(12.) But why do I address these obvious observations to you, my dear friend, when I am fully aware that they are quite familiar to your mind? I will tell you candidly why: because, though I have read not only with pleasure but with admiration your *Rationale* of Religion, I still more than doubt that you have allowed the principles on which we both agree to lead you into all the legitimate inferences which follow from them. You still take upon yourself to deny the name of Christians to men who claim it, only because their views do not fully agree with your own; you make a harsh declaration against certain divines whom you describe as *Rationalists*. Now, if by Rationalist you mean an expounder of the Scriptures who attempts to explain the miraculous narratives conjecturally by natural means, I, for one, will join you in declaring such an attempt as *generally* unsuccessful; but this is merely an exegetic question: I myself feel convinced that such a method of interpretation is unsatisfactory in by far the greater number of cases. Yet, if the liberties taken with the historical documents of the Bible were still much greater than those of the Rationalists, I would contend that no man has a right to deny the name of Christian to another who wishes to be known by that name, as long as it cannot be proved that he assumes it maliciously and for the purpose of deception. To declare any one unworthy of the name of Christian because he does not agree with your *belief*, is to fall into the intolerance of the Articled Churches. The moment that the name *Christian* is made necessarily to contain in its signification belief in certain historical or metaphysical propositions, that moment the name itself becomes a *creed:* the length of that creed is of little consequence.

"(13.) In vain will it be said that, according to this view, the signification of the word Christianity may be reduced to a kind of negative quantity: such an objection assumes the great point in question,—namely, that Christ left a *positive* creed to be indispensably accepted by all his disciples. Until such a fact shall be proved, no man has a right to reject another from the Christian union on account of any abstract opinion whatever. Christ's disciples were not known by the name of Christians till it was given to them, as it would appear, by the public at Antioch. This fact is important, because it prevents verbal subtleties as to the original signification of that word. Christian was a *popular* name, which the disciples accepted as one which avoided the invidiousness and contempt implied by the earlier one of *Nazarenes*. Thus it appears that *Christian* cannot be said to have had a scriptural sense; for, properly speaking, it is not scriptural. A *Christian* was originally (and should always continue to be) the designation of one who separated himself from Judaism and Heathenism, and joined the followers of Christ. Of the *reality* of his Christianity none could properly judge; for, according to the views of the primitive Christians attested by Paul, those alone were properly disciples who shewed in the temper of their minds that they were under the guidance of a moral spirit similar to that of Christ. It is the *priestly* spirit, the spirit of hierarchical association, which has attached the idea of assent to certain dogmas to the name of *Christian*.

"(14.) Nevertheless, the priesthoods have not entirely succeeded in that work; the unsophisticated mass of laymen, when shocked by the appellation of heretic (in such countries as Spain and Italy), and of infidel (in England), do not derive their feeling of disgust and horror from the idea of doctrines denied by the heretic or infidel, but from a conviction that those words imply an unprincipled and immoral conduct. Imagine, for instance, the impression which would be produced upon a servant, especially a well-inclined and modest woman, who being on the point of entering the family of a *Rationalist*, were to hear from a respectable divine, that though the person in question was an honourable man, unfortunately he was not a *Christian*. You will very naturally say, that no one but a fiery enthusiast would use such language: I certainly agree with you: but the necessity which I believe you acknowledge of not using it in common parlance, shews the evil of employing it theologically.

"(15.) Whatever errors may have crept in among the simple yet sublime views published by Christ, the practical moral character of his Gospel has always stood prominently above the abstract doctrines. From the first publication of Christianity to this very day, it may be safely asserted, that no sincere convert has embraced it, allured by its creed. A longing after 'whatsoever things are true, whatsoever things are honest, whatsoever things are just, whatsoever things are lovely, whatsoever things are of good report,' will be found more or less to be the motive of every original or renewed attempt to be a *Christian*. There is therefore a great moral responsibility in every discouragement placed in the way of such moral impressions as induce men to cling to the name and title of Christians. An attachment to that denomination should be fostered by every friend of human virtue, as being, unquestionably among Europeans, the most evident sign of a living moral principle in the soul.

"(16.) Let us then anxiously reject every remnant of that hierarchical, that thoroughly priestly spirit, which cares for no virtue which does not bear the seal and impress of a certain Church. Let us follow the example of Christ in rejecting none who approached him. Such traits of benevolent liberality, which abound in the Gospels, cannot *rationally* be suspected as being part of that superstructure of pious fraud which the early Christian priesthood began, and which their successors carried up to a monstrous height. The genuine views of Christ, the only true Christianity, will never combine with the hierarchical dogmas, so as to be undistinguishable. Christ's mission was evidently a *reform*, compared with the *positive* or preceptive and ceremonial religions then in existence. The 'Gospel of God's kingdom' may be correctly called a *negative* system. Christ published the religion of *conscience*, which, though essentially grounded upon the nature of man, and having faithful disciples at all times and in all nations, those men who, being without a written law, 'were a law to themselves,' and were just before God, 'because they obeyed the law written in their hearts, their conscience also bearing witness,'—had been obscured, and almost placed beyond the mental reach of the mass of mankind. Christ declared himself against all religions which made salvation, or spiritual safety, dependent on a priesthood and its peculiar offices. Hence the insurmountable difficulty with which all *successors*, and especially the Episcopal Protestants, have to contend; for if salvation must be dispensed to mankind through the hands of a *legitimate* priesthood, the world must be in a sad case as long as the titles shall continue in a state of the most hopeless litigation.

"(17.) What shall we say, then, of the still greater difficulty of finding the *learned* portion of Christianity, —that catalogue of historical and metaphysical propositions which every man is supposed to be concerned in, as he is concerned in his eternal happiness? Can a Christianity, containing a philosophical and critical department, be believed to have originated in that Jesus of Nazareth, whose anti-hierarchical and anti-rabbinical mental portrait is still transparent through the thick coating of sophistical and pharisaical paint which was spread over it before the middle of the second century?

"(18.) The practical meaning which the name Christian still preserves in the popular language of all Christian nations,—that fact to which I have already alluded, is to me a remarkable instance of the indestructible character of certain popular traditions. The Christian priesthoods have exerted themselves for ages in making people believe that the essence of Christianity consists in the belief of doctrines; yet the great currency which that notion obtained, arose exclusively from the *practical* shape in which it was preached. It was not assent to certain propositions, or belief in certain facts, that Christianity was said to demand; but *obedience* to the Church, and implicit trust in her doctrines. This is indeed an intelligible demand, which by the assistance of certain texts of Scripture has been recognized for ages by the great majority of the Christian world. The supposition that Christ had laid this duty upon all his future disciples is not absurd in itself; it is totally devoid of proof: but of this the mass of Christians are not sufficiently enlightened judges: such a submission is, indeed, much in accordance with the popular notions of religion among mankind; for a religion without a priesthood was scarcely conceived before Christ. But the idea of Christianity consisting pre-eminently of personal belief in, and of real conviction of, the truth of certain metaphysical tenets and certain historical facts,—this conviction to be grounded on the laws of historical criticism, on the intrinsic validity of certain documents, and the accuracy of their interpretation,—such Christianity, such method of spiritual safety, does not, cannot exist as a popular, much less as a universal religion. The mass of people who call themselves, and (I am ready to grant) are Christians in proportion to the sincerity of their wish to live according to their notions of Christ, have no more reason to be convinced of the authenticity of the Bible, than the people of Ephesus had in their day that the statue of the great Diana had fallen from heaven. Even most of those who have read such works as Paley's (a number, comparatively speaking, very small) cannot be said to believe in consequence of a fair examination of the case: such an examination would require the attentive perusal of the most accredited works of infidels. Such deliberate, impartial, and attentive hearing of both sides, would be necessary for a well-grounded decision. How then, I will ask, can it be supposed that Christ could have founded his universal religion upon such a basis? The Christian world,—the mass of Christians,—have never conceived anything of the kind; they think it one of their duties to treat the Bible as a book from heaven: this is part of their practical religion. Among Roman Catholics, this duty is a branch of obedience to the Church; among Protestants, an early inculcated habit; but in neither case will the great majority pretend that they have or ought to have a rational ground of conviction.

"(19.) What strange notions of God must lie at the bottom of such systems of Christianity as make eternal happiness depend on an *historical* faith!—an historical faith, too, of miraculous facts, of facts externally alike to those which, in all other histories out of the Bible, have been long stamped by all sensible historians as pure fables! I do not mean to rank *all* the miracles of the Bible with the mythico-historical narratives of the early history of every nation; I only wish the *external* similarity to be remarked; because, owing to that likeness, consisting of all that strikes the imagination, the work of discriminating and weighing the evidence for a *true* miracle must be confessed to be of the most difficult nature. Nevertheless, this work of thought and profound research is supposed to be made the condition of eternal happiness by the good and gracious Father of all mankind. Observe, however, the partiality implied in such a system. The difficulty of *historical* conviction is all for the thinking part of mankind; among whom miracles become more and more difficult of proof, in proportion as the knowledge of nature on the one hand, and of the character of historical documents on the other, increases. Here, however, we are told that this apparent partiality in favour of the 'poor and humble,' is the due reward of their moral temper. But the evasion is such, that were it not for the total want of reflection which attends all mysticism of this kind, few would not be ashamed to avow it; for it is obvious that the advantage in question belongs equally to the mentally indolent, to the mere man of the senses who detests the labour and fatigue of attention. This is practically exhibited every day before our eyes, though not so strikingly and abundantly as it appears in the history of the most brutal and immoral times, the ages of faith and violence, of devotion and profligacy,—the period of chivalry. When did the 'poor and humble' equal the barons and knights of those times in strong, unhesitating belief of the Bible, or of anything which they were told that it was *pious* and

Christian-like to believe? What candid man will deny, that if the main condition of Christianity is unhesitating belief in historical testimony, the kingdom of heaven announced by Christ belongs as an inheritance to the class of men to whose lot the possession of the earth has generally fallen; whilst the purest models of god-like humanity, those in whose composition the highest gifts of God,—intellect and reason,—predominate, must at all times, but especially in our own, and in the fast approaching ages of widely-spread thought, belong almost by a natural right to the 'devil and his angels'? This may be broadly expressed, I confess; but is it not the unvarnished substance of the doctrine maintained by all *articled* Churches; the doctrine to the root, at least, of which, I fear, not a few among us still cling, unaware that they do so?

"(20.) There is indeed only one way of getting safely out of this insecure position. The following question must be thoroughly examined and settled, with a manful and truly Christian indifference to obloquy; for that all the consequences of alarming inveterate prejudice will follow from such a bold examination, no one can doubt who knows the nature of superstition. Such, indeed, is its power, that I foresee a difficulty even in making the question which I propose intelligible to persons tainted with the existing *bibliolatry*. But I will do my best to be clear. The question is this:—

"Is it a Christian's duty, as such Christian, to receive as true whatever may be proved by the text of our Bibles to have been considered as true by the writers, some of whose works are contained in it? In other words, are we bound as Christians to believe—1st, that the writers of all and each of the books in the Bible were miraculously preserved from all error, or at least from errors connected with some kind of subjects, which we may clearly distinguish from all other subjects, so that we may be sure of the author's infallibility when he speaks about them? 2ndly. Are we bound as Christians to believe with the utmost assurance that the existing books of the Bible are the identical compositions which those writers left to the world, and that no curtailment, addition, or interpolation, has taken place in regard to those books?

"(21.) Here it will be absolutely necessary, as an indispensable previous step, to agree upon some general principles, without establishing which we cannot expect anything but pure wrangling. I conceive, then, that such an obligation in regard to the Bible should not be proved by *inference*. As I have already suggested, such an obligation cannot be established except by a clear and positive command of God. The existence of such a command should, besides, be made clear by those who contend for the above-mentioned obligation. Those who, as myself, deny it, are not bound to prove the *non-existence* of the divine command. The state of the question is, in fact, just the same as that of the infallibility of the Church. The Church must prove its title, not by inference, but positively and directly: he that denies that infallibility is not bound to prove by direct argument that it has not been granted: the want of a clear title to it is a sufficient proof.

"(22.) I also would demand, as a previous fundamental principle, that no injury to the consequences of the supposed privilege be alleged as a proof of its existence.

I cannot find a more effectual method of making this very important principle appear in a clear light than that of imagining ourselves among the contemporaries of Luther's Reformation, and considering the impression which arguments similar to those which my rule would exclude, would make upon the generality of the people. We should remember that the whole of that system of religion which we call Popery had grown out of two suppositions: 1st, that the salvation of mankind depended upon acquiescence in certain doctrines as *true*, and upon the admission of certain historical facts as *real:* 2nd, that there existed means, suited to the capacity of all men, not to mistake the sense of the books to which those doctrines were believed to have been consigned by God himself, and to prevent all doubt as to the miraculous nature of those books. The mainspring of this mighty machinery was the Church, which, having been for many centuries at work, had raised a mighty structure of dogmas and ceremonies, long identified with Christianity in the minds of all people. Habit must, in all such cases, give to the *growth* of the original false assumption the appearance of a *final end*, while its root, —the gratuitous assumption, takes the character of means totally indispensable for the attainment of the imaginary end. Now, under such circumstances, it will always happen that whenever the root of the evil is touched,—whenever its legitimacy is questioned,—no arguments are more popularly conclusive against the objectors than those which go to prove that the system which long custom has consecrated cannot stand without the ground now assailed. There cannot be a doubt that such arguments were the strongest barrier which checked the Reformation. 'You would make the Church fallible in matters of faith' (people would say with alarm and indignation); 'you would question her power to bind and to loose. How then can we be sure that our belief is not heretical; or how can we enjoy a comfortable assurance of the remission of our sins? Observe, besides (they would continue to object), the innumerable cases in which the Pope's dispensing power is required: what shall we do without it in the multitude of complicated events which no law can provide for?' I cannot conceive anything more powerful than this reasoning to excite a general feeling of abhorrence to the Reformation. Whence, I ask, does the fallacy derive its strong power of delusion? From a mere winking the principle, the recognition of which I contend for: the fallacy derives its power from the circumstance that the *growth* or the consequences of the assailed assumption are regarded as important *final ends*, and the false assumption itself is defended upon the score of its being indispensable for the attainment of those ends. It is perfectly true, whatever the *orthodox* Protestants may say, that without an infallible Church, *salvation* by means of an orthodox creed hangs upon a desperate chance; but if the notion of a salvation which depends on orthodoxy is the *growth* of hierarchical pretensions ignorantly admitted at first, and subsequently confirmed by superstition, habit, and violence, the objection that if we reject the *infallibility of the Church*, we cannot rest our orthodoxy upon the *infallibility of the Church*, is quite ludicrous. Let us then beware of a similar reasoning respecting the oracular character of the Scriptures. To object that, if the Scriptures are not infallible, we cannot have an infallible foundation for our religious creed, is just such an argument as I have stated in favour of Church infallibility. The necessity of infallibility in religion must first be proved to exist; if this cannot be done, we must not be surprised by the discovery that God has not given us the means of attaining what he has not demanded.

"(23.) Exactly of the same logical character is the objection, that such *rationalism* as I contend for renders useless all God's revelations to man. 'If the Bible (it will be said) is to be treated like any other collection of writings, we must at once make up our minds to the melancholy state of being without a direct means of knowing the will of God,—we must acknowledge that we have no advantage over the heathen world.' Here, again, the failure of results which were expected upon a false assumption, is charged upon those who shew that the assumption is groundless. It has been assumed that if the Bible is inspired, mankind are brought by means of it nearer to the Deity than they have been, and must remain, in case such inspiration cannot be proved; but any one who shall shew the fallacies upon which the supposition was made, will be sure to be accused of the cruelty and impiety of destroying the only means of direct communication with God. I do not mention this as a peculiar hardship to which I myself must submit. At all times and in all places, he who ventures to disturb a flattering delusion will be described as a wanton aggressor, as an enemy to the happiness of his fellow-men. Thank Heaven, the frequent and melancholy disappointments which the more civilized part of the world have experienced on such subjects, have opened the eyes of a sufficient number to diminish the danger of those whose unwelcome vocation is to contend with popular delusions.

"(24.) In the present case I might content myself with an appeal to the long and varied experience which shews that the theory of inspiration (especially among Protestants) totally fails of the results for the sake of which it has been set forth. But I wish to attack the root itself of the delusion. In my view of the subject, even the most direct and personal communication with God of any writer, could not give to his books the power of conveying a *supernatural*, or rather *superrational*, conviction to the readers. In establishing this important point, deep prejudice and trembling superstition present the only difficulties with which intellect has to contend. As, for the present, I totally despair of gaining any ground, I shall only point to principles on which men accustomed to follow reason in spite of imagination, will, I trust, readily agree with me.

"The notion of a certainty above reason,—a *superrational* certainty I wish to call it,—is so self-contradictory, that it cannot be well conceived by the mind. Yet such a notion is the only foundation of the established *supernaturalism*. With a truly infantine ignorance of man's mental constitution, people continue to imagine that no belief can exceed in certainty that which would arise from hearing God himself make a verbal statement of what he wished mankind to hold as unquestionably true. But there is a monstrous misconception at the bottom of this notion; for does it not suppose that God may make himself an object of which our senses may judge? God, I doubt not, can do all things, except what is in contradiction with himself: it is he who has made our senses in such a manner that they can receive only certain kind of impressions,—impressions essentially distinct from everything mental or spiritual. The supposition then that he would resort to such a medium for a more immediate and more secure communication with man, implies a charge of ignorance of his own works in the great Creator. 'God is a Spirit,' is the sublime fundamental principle of Christ's religion. Man, too, is in part a spirit; and the communication between the spiritual Creator and that visible creature of his who bears the *spiritual* stamp of his likeness, would naturally be expected to be between the two spirits,—the spirit of God and the spirit in man. But no: this could not take place except through man's reason; and that supreme power within us is said to be too weak, too much exposed to error and delusion. How shall this difficulty be obviated? How shall God remove uncertainty from his most particular and important communications with man? 'Let God be seen and heard,' answers the supernaturalist. In vain it is declared (though it scarcely needed a declaration) that 'no man has seen God at any time.' The divine will confidently explain away this assertion, and tell us that God was frequently seen in the time of the patriarchs, and was distinctly heard by the whole people of Israel. Reason, he tells us, is a deceitful guide: but here, it seems, there was no room for mistake,—a mountain was seen in flames,—there was an earthquake,—a trumpet sounded,—and a voice was heard speaking distinctly. Such, we are told, is one of the most remarkable instances of direct communication between God and man intended to obviate the danger of our being misled by reason, and to establish a certainty in religious matters for all ages and nations to come. This is to be considered a source of certainty above all assurance which could be obtained *spiritually*, or, what is the same, *rationally*. But let us see: God spoke: are we sure that God has a voice, or that when a sound like that of the human voice cannot be traced to any man, it must, beyond all doubt, originate in God? The world has been full of delusions, bearing internal marks very like the communication in question. I will not say that this is a delusion of the same kind as those which are recorded in profane history; but the *senses* are subject to delusions; and how can we be *certain* that the witnesses of such manifestations of God through the senses took every reasonable precaution against mistake? But I will not tire you with a minute enumeration of the doubts which inevitably surround a transaction of this kind, as soon as it is consigned to history, in order (it is supposed) to produce a *superrational* conviction, at the distance of an indefinite number of years. It seems quite incredible that such an ignorance of ourselves, of our faculties, of the grounds of our conviction, as is betrayed in the above supposition, should exist among us. God, in the first place, is asserted to have addressed himself to the external senses of man, distrusting the powers which he had imparted to man's mind. Such, we are told, was the Deity's pre-eminent means of giving us certainty upon things on which our eternal well-being depended. But it is clear that all this contrivance of ocular and auricular certainty could reach only those whose eyes and ears were affected at a certain time.

The benefit of that supposed certainty was confined to a small number of men, upon a very limited spot. What then is to be the ground of certainty for the millions of millions, equally concerned in the subject, who were not present? 'Historical evidence,' we are told, 'is enough for *them*.' But historical evidence, however complete and strong, does not address itself to the senses, which the supernaturalist makes the vehicles of the highest certainty,—certainty above that of which reason is capable. What we and all the rest of mankind, except the witnesses of a miracle, can examine by means of our senses, are writings which can prove nothing, except by the help and under the approbation of reason. The credibility of the witnesses, the authenticity of the documents, their perfect agreement with the original manuscripts,—are these things objects of sense? Unquestionably not: the blindest enthusiast must confess that reason is here to be the judge; and since its approbation must be at the bottom of the whole process, even the blindest enthusiast, if he still preserves common sense undisturbed in the slightest degree, must confess that the supposed divine contrivance to avoid the fallibility of human reason, has totally failed; and that the originally discarded reason must be the foundation of belief in those miracles which were intended to supersede it in matters, as they are called, of revelation.

"(25.) Verbal revelation and miracles have for ages been treated under the false notion which I have just laid before you. Both have been, most unphilosophically, imagined to be *evidence* above reason. Such an error would not find admittance even into our nurseries, if a most tyrannical power, supported by the popular errors it creates and cherishes, had not transmitted, through a long series of generations, an inheritance of mental servility of which hardly our children's children will be totally free. I wish you to imagine what would be the conduct of truly pious and unenthusiastic men in the present day, if a case of resurrection by miracle was to appear in the public journals. In the first place, there would be an extreme reluctance to pay any serious regard to the statement. Whence, I ask, this reluctance to examine into modern miracles? Surely the evidence adduced for some of the cures of Prince Hohenlohe is not, *primâ facie*, contemptible. Still, the stoutest believers of the miraculous in the Bible, would, if Protestants, look with a feeling less respectful than pity on any one, not a Roman Catholic, who should undertake a journey for the purpose of examining the evidence of the alleged miracle upon the spot. This mental fact, this reluctance to give credit to miraculous transactions, and the law of its appearance and growth, are things not to be overlooked in the present question. Bold indeed must be that ignorance which shall attribute it to individual perverseness. Few mental phenomena can be better established, as inseparably connected with our intellectual nature, than the attraction of the miraculous in the infancy of mind, and its repulsiveness for the same mind instructed and developed. To man, in individual as well as in collective or national childhood, a miracle is evidence to itself; and the more extraordinary the miracle, the greater the certainty which a mere narrative of it will convey. Ramahoun Roy's experience coincides here most satisfactorily with theory; he has, as I remember, stated somewhere that missionaries can produce no impression upon the Hindoos by means of the Bible miracles. Accustomed to the extravagant magnitude of their own wonders, they smile upon the insignificance of ours. Nor can any one be surprised at this, considering that whatever makes a deep impression upon the imaginative faculty, is in that state of the human mind taken for absolute reality; consequently the narrative of the miracle, which leaves deeper traces upon the fancy than that of a more modest and unambitious wonder, must indispose the undeveloped mind for a belief in the latter. Such, then, being the immutable laws of the human understanding, the Eternal Source of those laws, if he intended to guide mankind by *miracles* (and verbal revelation is of that class), not by reason, must have intended two things: First, that the great mass of mankind in a low state of mental development should follow the most extravagant dreams of enthusiasm and imposture. Secondly, that in proportion as the human mind increased in knowledge, so it would reject the miraculous divine guidance. I have examined this objection to the common theological notions on revelation and miracles, with the utmost impartiality and attention of which I am capable; I have done so for many years, under a desire of finding it fallacious; for the superstitious fears inspired by my early education were not easily subdued; but I never could discover even a plausible answer.

" (26.) What I am about to say, is a result of the same inquiry, and by no means one of the concessions which the opponents of religious prejudices frequently make for the sake of allaying the alarm which their too unceremonious approach to the popular idols may have raised.

In the course of my examination of verbal revelation and miracles, I have found no convincing reason for denying that God may have, on some occasions, put forth energies which do not belong to the system of regular and invariable forces by which he conducts the phenomena of nature. But I see no ground whatever for believing that such extraordinary instances of *occasional* divine activity had human belief for their object. If God has at any time acted visibly, either against or beyond the range of the laws which he gave to his creation, he certainly must have done it for the sake of the thing thus performed, and not to give rise to historical or traditional narratives to be believed in distant times. Within the narrow limits of the probability which these matters admit, I believe that, besides that immediate divine energy attested by the recent existence of man on the face of this globe, the preservation of the parents of mankind, immediately after their formation, was an effect not within the reach of the existing natural laws. Admitting the immediate formation of one or more couples, especially of the lower classes of animals, endowed at once with the instincts which belong to their species, we may well conceive the manner in which they would preserve themselves and propagate their race. But man possesses no such instincts: and if we imagine one or more couples formed at once in a state of full development, and then left to themselves, it will not be easy to conjecture by what *natural* means, within the existing laws, they could be preserved. We know how long infants are in learning to see,—to measure distances,—to use their hands,—and to walk. It seems indeed very probable that the acquisition of these powers would be still more difficult to a human being who (by supposition) should have to obtain them when his body had attained full growth. The provision of food for the grown infants, which the fact of creation forces us to admit, must have been made by an individual act of the creating power, since the wonderful means provided by the law of procreation are totally excluded in the case before us. So far, I am willing to admit, there is a strong *conjectural* ground for the existence of a divine operation, which, like creation itself, may be well ranked as a miracle; yet not a miracle for show (as the etymology of that word implies), but one which might be considered as a personal act out of the reach of the laws, whose operation could not commence but subsequently to that act. In a mental point of view, that is, in relation to the human mind, this conjecture affords a valuable support to the various grounds upon which our race, after having emerged from that low state of intellect which produces idolatry and anthropomorphism, may, in such ages as the present, preserve itself from pantheism, or the belief of an impersonal Creator,—a necessarily constructive, but unconscious Deity.

"(27.) In regard to what is called *revelation* (which, to avoid ambiguity, I shall define a personal teaching of an individual man by God), I feel confident that the established notions are perfectly untenable. Those notions belong to a period of imperfect development, and, as it has been already shewn, arise from a gross mistake regarding the nature of belief and of evidence. This has been more or less clearly perceived, even in ages when the belief in visions and verbal communications from an invisible world was totally unshaken. We find common sense breaking out and betraying its first perception of the inadequacy of visions and miracles to establish truth, in the Old Testament itself. Manoah, for instance, insists upon having his own tests applied to the heavenly vision, that he may be sure of the reality of a heavenly message. I cannot at this moment bring to my recollection other instances of the same kind, though I believe they are to be found in the Bible; but the suspicion of delusion is so natural, so thoroughly grounded in nature, that men appear to be unable to feel secure against it, except when, being cautioned to be upon their guard on that point, superstition makes them at once impenetrable to argument. Hence it is that in appeals to nature, especially to that nature which is best known to consciousness (I wish to speak without personal offence), the very name of theology deprives me of confidence; for theology, as it is studied among us generally, stifles the voice of nature within, and few, even under the most sincere wish to listen to it, can perceive its still small voice, drowned as it is by the loud and harsh cries of authority. It is fortunate indeed, in such a case, to have an attestation from Nature herself, through one of her most unprejudiced and distinguished favourites. Hear it then in the following lines:—

> 'The spirit that I have seen
> May be a devil, and the devil hath power
> To assume a pleasing shape; yea, and perhaps,
> Out of my meekness and my melancholy
> (As he is very potent with such spirits),
> Abuses me to damn me. *I'll have grounds
> More relative than this.*'

The greatest interpreter of Nature has given us here her

eternal, immutable answer to the claims of visions and miracles to be the foundations of religious truth. I will not, as I have said of miracles (for there is no essential difference between the two things in question), I will not assert that God has never used some extraordinary impressions on the senses as means of drawing attention to important truths, or rather of inclining the will of the rude and unthinking multitude to follow the dictates of those whom he had endowed with the high moral and intellectual qualities which *truly* distinguish his messengers for good to man. But in matters of truth,

> 'I'll have grounds
> More relative than this.'

The only safe grounds are those essentially connected with the truth to be received. That all external phenomena, all impressions on the senses, are *irrelative* to spiritual truth, is proved by the crowd of impressions *deemed miraculous* which the successive generations which have peopled, and at this moment inhabit, this globe, make their ground for belief in the most monstrous errors. Let us, my dear friend, have *grounds more relative* for what we embrace as pure Christianity.

"(28.) And it is very remarkable that all thinking men, however prepossessed in favour of miraculous evidence, look for proofs *more relative* to the truths in which they feel a deep interest. This appears in the unconcern with which they treat all miracles alleged against their settled belief. Now, if their reason were thoroughly satisfied that miracles are the most unquestionable stamp of divine communications, honest men would not be so inconsistent as to turn away disdainfully from modern miracles; nay, they would take sufficient pains to weigh the evidence of the miracles which support the unhesitating religious belief of other sects and other nations. Let the supernaturalist be just upon such an important point; let him put aside that national pride, and that more extended though weaker pride of race, which stand to him in lieu of examination for his comfortable conviction that all miracles but the Jewish and Christian are totally unworthy of attention. A man whose religious belief is founded upon the intrinsic and rational worth of what he embraces as such,—he who is perfectly convinced that what most concerns every individual man, must have been placed by the great Creator within the reach of our mind, if it but honestly wish to exert its faculties,—such a man may justly turn a deaf ear to those who call him to examine the various and reciprocally-opposed collections of miraculous evidence, ancient and modern; for he is convinced that God has not appointed that kind of evidence for those, at least, to whom he has not addressed it in itself and originally : but it is most unreasonable, not to say arrogant, in those who contend that miraculous evidence, *reduced to testimony*, is the direct and the highest proof of revealed truth, to sit down contentedly in their own corner of the world, closing their eyes to all other evidence of the same kind. Protestants of this description are bound, at the least, to go to Rome, and examine the detailed evidence of thousands of miracles proved to the satisfaction of a board of cardinals, who pass judgment in conformity with a previously-established code of laws. Many a smile, and many a scowl too, will be raised on hearing this invitation; but what will the smilers and the scowlers say to a similar answer from a follower of Mahomet, or of Brahma, on their being invited to examine the miraculous evidence of the Bible? I, for one, well know what my address would be on such occasion. I would desire the Mahometan, the Hindoo, and all others, to reflect on the view of religion which I myself call Christianity,—to compare it with his national religion, and judge between the two. If he appealed to the wonders exhibited in past ages, I would tell him that, in my relative ignorance of Oriental history, and total unacquaintance with the language of the documents adduced as the testimony of ocular witnesses of his national miracles, I could not judge their value and weight. I would mention the Christian Scriptures, and my just confidence in their intrinsic value, just to make him perceive the analogy of our respective situations in regard to the written testimony of past ages. From the certainty of this analogy, from the obviously insuperable difficulty of his transforming himself into a European scholar, or my becoming a learned Pundit, in good time for making up our minds on the respective value of our traditional evidence of miracles, I hope I could infer satisfactorily for a reasonable man of any nation whatever, that God cannot have made our happiness depend upon the settlement of such a question. Having conjured away that disturbing mental phantom, the rest of the examination could not fail to be both improving and satisfactory to any couple of upright men, whatever might be their respective conclusions at the end of the conference.

"(29.) Is this *Rationalism*, or is it already rank infidelity,—a formal renunciation of all revelation? I confess I am perfectly indifferent to the name by which others may choose to express the simple fact that they do not agree with me. But I am far from being indifferent to the removal of dark and unsocial prejudices, when there is a chance left of my being heard on these important subjects. I wish, therefore, to request the serious attention of men not totally blinded by the spirit of Orthodoxy, to a passage in the Old Testament which clearly proves the inferior value, as evidence, which Moses, or whoever was the writer of the book of Deuteronomy, sets on miracles. The too common practice of talking a great deal of the inspiration of the Old Testament, whilst by some it is read in detached passages merely as a charm, and in total indifference to the sense; and by others it is kept as much as possible out of view, in order to avoid the disturbance which, if read attentively, it never fails to produce in the minds of thinking persons,—this practice alone is the cause of the general notion that the Bible lays the ultimate foundation of religion on miracle. The following passage deserves deliberate attention: it is in the 13th chapter of Deuteronomy:

"'If there arise among you a prophet or a dreamer of dreams, and giveth thee a sign or a wonder, and the sign or the wonder come to pass, whereof he spake unto thee, saying, Let us go after other gods, which thou hast not known, and let us serve them; thou shalt not hearken unto the words of that prophet, or of that dreamer of dreams: for the Lord your God proveth you, to know whether ye love the Lord your God with all your heart and with all your soul. Ye shall walk after the Lord your God and fear him, and keep his commandments and obey his voice, and ye shall serve him, and cleave unto him.

And that prophet, or that dreamer of dreams, shall be put to death.'

"This *rationale* of miraculous evidence deserves a degree of consideration from those who conceive *revelation* to depend on miracles, which they certainly have not bestowed upon it. It discloses something very extraordinary relating to God, but, at the same time, most important in regard to miraculous evidence. According to this oracular writer, God, after having established a religion by miracles, may happen to assist false prophets in the performance of really miraculous works,—or, at least, may connive at the production of signs and wonders perfectly undistinguishable from miracles, with a view to try whether a people's belief in their religion is proof against that same kind of evidence which made them embrace it. Now the question occurs, Did the Jews act upon this *revealed* command in regard to Christ? Unless they were accustomed to read the Old Testament like most divines among us, they could not have overlooked a law so obviously applicable to the miracles of Jesus and his apostles. Yet either the Christian documents have suppressed the very perplexing argument which this passage offered to the Scribes and Pharisees, or both Christ and his learned contemporaries must have been aware of the inherent and intrinsic weakness of miraculous evidence. There are, indeed, in the Gospels deeply-marked traces of Christ's dislike to the popular notions regarding miracles: the genuineness of the passages in which Jesus reproves the Jews for their determination not to believe him except on the ground of miraculous exhibitions, becomes unquestionable, when we consider that those speeches are preserved by men who fully partook of the popular notions in favour of miraculous proofs of doctrine, of men who evidently did not understand the meaning of such sayings, nor their inconsistency with the abundance of miracles found in their narratives. But I leave those who *ground* their Christianity on miracles and inspired books to grapple with these difficulties. One thing after all is evident,— that the Bible itself is not *decidedly* in favour of the notion that the *miraculous* can be the ultimate proof of a divine revelation. As to Christ himself, a conviction that miracles must be the credentials of an extraordinary messenger from God, is totally inconsistent with his reproof to the Jews,—'Except you see signs and wonders, you will not believe.' If we follow up the consequences of the commonly-established notions on this subject, the Jews were perfectly right in not believing except under that condition. But, in justice to them, it must be acknowledged that not even the clearest miracles could relieve them from a most distressing perplexity; the book of Deuteronomy excludes all miraculous evidence in regard to the Jews themselves, and condemns the miracle-worker to death. The Jew was bound to continue what he was in regard to religion, even if heaven and earth obeyed the voice of a reforming prophet: the sun might rise in the west, and the seasons change their succession at his command. The Jew,—the faithful, orthodox Jew,—would not be moved at such signs, for he had the highest authority to believe '*that the Lord his God was proving* him.' Such was his clear duty, according to the Law, even when the miracles were worked before his eyes. What then can be expected from the conscientious Israelite of our own times, who has only miracles *in writing* to convince him?

"(30.) What then, I shall be asked, can prove a revelation from heaven? I know nothing that can prove it except the thing revealed. How the glorious thoughts, pregnant with blessings to mankind, were imparted by the Father of lights 'at sundry times and in divers manners,' but especially 'in these last days' to his greatest messenger, Christ,—whether those thoughts arose according to the established laws of mind, or were breathed, together with a vivifying moral spirit, into the souls of the divine messengers, we have not means to ascertain; all that we are enabled to do is to appreciate the value of the message itself. Revelation is precious because it communicates *truth*. Gold might be miraculously drawn from the bowels of the earth, but its miraculous origin could not raise its standard when put into circulation with other gold. The wisdom of God, I doubt not, has, in mercy to mankind, chosen instructors, whom, by means known to God alone, he has enabled to do for the world what, as far as we can judge, would be out of the power of any individual unsupported by a peculiar divine assistance. Among the benefactors of mankind, I cannot find any one to compare to Jesus of Nazareth. But if mankind cannot be benefited by the truths he taught, except through an *historical* conviction that those truths were miraculously known and miraculously proved, the truly divine mission of Christ is doomed to remain without anything like an adequate result. Millions of men may continue to call themselves Christians, but with no more reason than they would be called Mahometans, if chance had united that name with the circumstances of their birth and education. Unless Christianity be what men, all over the world, may *rationally* accept as soon as education shall have awakened their *conscientious reason*,—that faculty which judges between moral evil and good,—unless Christianity can be preached *to the poor* without the assistance either of enthusiasm, or of *historical* and *critical* proofs,—we are forced to conclude that either Christ mistook the nature of his own religion, or that his followers have perfectly disqualified it to answer the purpose of universality for which he intended it. I know that it will be said that the great mass of mankind are very imperfect judges of moral truth. I answer, that there is a still greater mass who are much less qualified to judge of historical truth. I cannot conceive how the idea that Christianity must derive all its efficacy as *history*, can maintain its hold on any mind tolerably acquainted with the character of historical testimony. 'Historical testimony in support of events analogous to those with which a universal experience acquaints us, is above the judgment of the generality of people. None but thoroughly educated men who have paid a particular attention to historical criticism, can properly estimate the authority of the documents from which the history of England, for instance, or of France, is derived. How strange then is the supposition that every one who calls himself a Christian is capable of understanding the reasons upon which it is asserted that the existing historical testimony to the reality of the Bible miracles is sufficient! An ingenious answer has been lately given to this difficulty by my excellent friend Dr. H * * *, who says, 'that it is enough for the mass of the people to know that the authenticity of the Christian documents has stood the attacks of the unbelieving writers.' But how do they know this, except through the controversialists on their own side? How can they be sure that, while the law of the land threatens with severe punishment any one who in a publication should conclude against the authenticity of any considerable part of the Bible, there are not many among those on whose authority they rely who secretly believe that the German critics of the Rationalist school (as they are called) have had the best of the argument? I cannot conceive how any unprejudiced person to whom the difficulties of historical proof are known, can deliberately assert that the great mass of mankind of all countries and ages can receive Christianity upon historical grounds, especially if upon such grounds it be their duty to believe in the miracles both of the Old and the New Testament!

"I have, my dear friend, been writing on, day by day, and only for a very short period each time, for my health has been, and continues, much worse than usual. I fear, therefore, that you will find it difficult to collect any clear and distinct general notion from the rambling thoughts which I have already consigned to this letter; as my strength does not allow me to re-cast it, and reduce what I have said into one clear and distinct view, I must take the liberty of sending to you this rather loose collection of notes, requesting your attentive consideration of them individually. It is of great importance to ascertain whether these objections to some deeply-rooted notions which exist among all denominations of Christians are as valid as I think, or not. [The only method by which we can arrive at a perfect knowledge of the object of Providence in the unquestionably great work which began with our era, and has uninterruptedly proceeded up to the moment when, in consequence of the moral impulse then given to a great portion of mankind, I am anxiously exerting myself on the subject of Christianity, —the only way to complete the Reformation which Luther proclaimed, is to remove, one by one, every false notion which we may find connected with the profession of the Gospel.] While employed in the removal of individual errors, we should be upon our guard against the usual bugbear, 'Where shall we stop?'—'What will be left?' When we shall have removed what is positively *not* Christianity, then, and not till then, shall we be able to perceive what *true* Christianity is.

"Ever, with sincere affection,
"Your friend and brother,
"J. BLANCO WHITE."

"The Rev. James Martineau."

CONTENTS.

	PAGE
Outlines of the Life of Joseph Blanco White, by John Hamilton Thom	iii
Funeral Address, by James Martineau	xxxix
Sonnet, by Joseph Blanco White	xliv

OBSERVATIONS ON HERESY AND ORTHODOXY.

Dedication, written in 1839	xlvii
Preface to the First Edition, 1835	lix

LETTER I.

A History of the *Inquisition* worse than useless if not preceded by a true definition of *Heresy*	2
Some latent error in the usual phrase *Christian truth*	4
Only true sense of the phrase *Christian truth*	5, 6
True meaning of the word *Heresy*, as used among Christians	7
Question on which the necessary existence of some degree of interference, like that claimed by the Papal Inquisition, or the absence of that claim, depends	7, 8, note
Protestantism, on the basis of Orthodoxy, untenable	8
Unanswerable arguments of the Roman Catholics against such Protestantism	9
Unanswerable arguments of the unbelievers against that Protestantism	10
If Christ and his Apostles, by *saving faith*, understood Orthodoxy, Christianity cannot be true	12
Proofs that such was not Christ's and Apostles' meaning of *faith*	13
True meaning of the word Faith	14
No judge of Orthodoxy appointed	15
Union of Christians not dependent on unity of abstract doctrines	16
Obvious means of establishing unity of doctrine on abstract points, if Christ had intended it, as the bond of his disciples	17
What must men agree upon to be Christians?	18
What kind of men are excluded by St. Paul and St. John	19, 20
Acceptance of Christ as supreme religious guide, the original condition of Christian communion	21
Natural sources of error connected with the only essential condition of Christian communion	22
Paul's notion of *Heresy*: exposition of part of 1st Cor. iii.	22—25

LETTER II.

	PAGE
Theological writers who do not follow the scholastic phraseology, in constant danger of being misunderstood	26
Passions which disturb the judgment of the generality of people attached to some theological system	27
Main argument of Letter I. collectively stated	28—33
Call of the Gospel made to the *will*	34
Essential difference between such a call and one made upon the *understanding*, especially in relation to the interpretation of language	34, 35
Unadulterated Christianity in perfect harmony with the nature of our moral being	36, 37
The *understanding* not morally responsible	38—40
Translation of 1st Cor. xiii. 12, corrected	40, note
Duty of *veracity*	40
Christians should not deceive each other as to the results of their respective perceptions of the sense of the Scriptures	41, 42
Advantages which Christianity would derive from a general faithfulness to the duty of *veracity*	43, 44
Unjustifiable methods of perpetuating certain interpretations of Scripture	44, 45
The *established orthodoxies* of the Christian world prevent our knowing the sense of the Scripture according to a successive and comparative experience of the various generations of Christians	45, 46
What the Church of Christ might be if its growth had not been perverted by Orthodoxy	47
Orthodoxy has placed the world in a worse condition for peace and charity than it was before the Gospel	48, 49
The reason of this explained	50
Gospel liberty	52
Mark xvi. 16, Matt. x. 14, 15, explained	53, note
Paul's notions of Christian liberty	54
Connection of the words SPIRIT and LIBERTY in the New Testament	57, 58

LETTER III.

Necessity of keeping in mind what has been proved, that *Heresy*, in the usual sense of the word, cannot exist unless there exists a divinely-appointed judge of controversies	60
Difficulty of uprooting errors arising from misapplied texts of Scripture	60, 61

CONTENTS.

	PAGE
Method of avoiding great mistakes in the interpretation of the New Testament	62
The sense of passages relating to speculative subjects cannot be obvious	62
Erroneous notions inculcated in early life make them less obvious than they might be	62
Certain passages of the New Testament recommended for the purpose of overcoming those mental habits	63
The 3rd chapter of 2nd Epistle to the Corinthians explained	64—66
That chapter opposed to the notion of Orthodoxy as necessary to salvation	67
The Scriptures were not appointed to be the rule of that pretended condition of salvation	68—72
The Scriptures addressed to *reason* as it resides in man	73, 74
Reason, as derived from God, is the "light which lighteth every man that cometh into the world"	75—77
The "carnal mind, which is enmity against God," is the opposite of *reason*	77
"Let us not therefore judge one another"	79

LETTER IV.

Scriptural signification of the word *Heresy*	80
Early causes of the misapplication of that word	81
Christianity taken up by speculatists as a basis for their theories	82—84
St. Paul's rivals belonged to the class of Judeo-philosophical speculatists	85
Proof of the former assertion in the character of Apollos	86, 87
Utility of abstract doctrines for the purpose of maintaining the self-importance of nominal Christian preachers	88
A specimen of the early sources of speculative corruptions	89
Some of the subsequent speculations, comparatively, not less absurd	90, 91
The Gospel, without Orthodoxy, what? True character and use of the New Testament	92—94
Power which Christian teachers derive from the supposed necessity of Orthodoxy	95
The notion of *saving* Orthodoxy necessarily intolerant	96
Steps by which the apostolical condemnation of *dissension* was transferred to *dissent*	97
Historical traces of early toleration among Christians	97
Organized tyranny of the Bishops which soon followed	100

LETTER V.

	PAGE
Reason charged with sin among Protestants	102
What can *pride of reason* be?	103—105
Why most languages want a word to express the virtuous feeling of which *pride*, in the common sense of that word, is an excess	106
Pride of reason defined	107
Pride of reason absurdly supposed to be a rebellion of reason against God	108
Mistake in which that notion originates	108, 109
Who are really guilty of *pride of reason*	110
Pride of sight, an illustration	111
Those who identify their own explanations of Scripture with the word of God are guilty of pride of reason	113
The spirit of Orthodoxy inseparable from *pride of reason*	114
The *Trinitarians* and the *Unitarians* compared in regard to *pride of reason*	114—116
Reluctance to believe what is directly against the first principles of reason, mistaken for *pride*	116, 117
The New Testament compared with the Orthodox system in regard to *reasonableness*	117—121
The Orthodox doctrines cannot be divested of their verbal mysteriousness without the *appearance* of scorn	122—124
Fallacy of comparing the mysteries of *Orthodoxy* and the mysteries of *Nature*	125—127
Difference between mysteries *to be explained* and *mysteries to be proved*	128
Dangerous position of orthodox Protestants, who cherish the root of Popery	129—132

APPENDICES.

I. On the omission of the article before the word *Christ*	133
II. Extracts from Professor Norton's Statement	137
III. A passage from Archdeacon Blackburne's *Confessional*	148
IV. On the Old Testament as a supposed standard of Orthodoxy	154

NOTES.

On 2nd John 7—11	159
On the word *Salvation*	162
On the spiritual assistance promised by Christ	163
On a passage from Fénélon	164

ADDITIONAL APPENDIX.

Letter from Rev. Joseph Blanco White to Rev. James Martineau	166

www.ingramcontent.com/pod-product-compliance
Lightning Source LLC
Chambersburg PA
CBHW031939230426
43672CB00010B/1984